F. Mason.

by **Paula Milne**

Editor **Linda Buckle**

The Television Literary Project

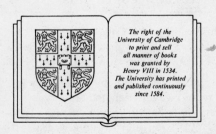

The right of the
University of Cambridge
to print and sell
all manner of books
was granted by
Henry VIII in 1534.
The University has printed
and published continuously
since 1584.

CAMBRIDGE UNIVERSITY PRESS

Cambridge

New York   New Rochelle   Melbourne   Sydney

Published by the Press Syndicate of the University of Cambridge
The Pitt Building, Trumpington Street, Cambridge CB2 1RP
32 East 57th Street, New York, NY 10022, USA
10 Stamford Road, Oakleigh, Melbourne 3166, Australia

First published 1988

Printed in Great Britain at the University Press, Cambridge

ISBN 0 521 35934 1

DS

A VHS videocassette of S.W.A.L.K. (containing all six episodes) is
available to schools and colleges through the following British
suppliers. (Please check for prices at the time of ordering.)

Concord Films Council Ltd
201 Felixstowe Road
Ipswich
Suffolk IP3 9BJ
(Videocassettes are also
available for hire.)

Cambridge University Press
(Home Sales Department)
The Edinburgh Building
Shaftesbury Road
Cambridge CB2 2RU

Acknowledgements

Front cover illustration: Nicola Cowper as Amanda in *S.W.A.L.K.*
(Thames Television) by Paula Milne; directed by Richard Bramall,
produced by Sheila Kinany, executive producer Pamela Lonsdale

The author and publisher are grateful to the following for
permission to reproduce copyright material:
Eileen McAuley, *The Seduction;*
Stevie Smith, 'Not Waving But Drowning' © 1957, from *Not Waving
But Drowning, Poems by Stevie Smith*, André Deutsch Ltd.

Contents

Introduction

Are women and men, girls and boys, really that different, or are they just treated differently by society and the people around them? What do you think?

Take a look at most people's attitudes towards babies from the moment they are born. Girls and boys are often dressed differently while still in the pram – boys in blue, girls in pink. Have you ever asked yourself why? Why does it matter what sex the child is? Usually the first question asked when a baby is born is whether it is a boy or a girl, and attitudes towards the child sometimes differ acording to the reply:

> 'What a pretty little thing you are!'
> 'Don't cry – boys don't cry!'

So before a baby can understand language we are already varying our response and attitude. We tend to force society's masculine attributes onto boys, and feminine qualities onto girls, right from the start. Little boys are often encouraged to be physically hardy and to repress emotion, whereas the opposite can be expected from girls. Look at the attitudes parents or relatives have towards you and any brothers or sisters you may have. Do they ever expect different standards of behaviour or give you different jobs to do around the house? Do you ever feel you are treated unfairly at home because of your sex? How might this affect the way you think and act as an adult, if you have been treated in this way as a child?

Girls and boys are usually given different toys to play with. Girls are often encouraged to become miniature copies of their mothers, and given prams and baby dolls and cleaning kits. Even seemingly neutral toys such as dolls may encourage an interest in dress and appearance in girls. Their brothers usually have building bricks, 'action men' and train-sets to play with. Look back at your early childhood – is this the kind of thing that happened to you? How do you think it has affected the way you are growing up and thinking?

This kind of consistent treatment from such an early age must have a big effect on how we see ourselves and how others look at us. Both sexes are pressurised into being typical males or females who view the opposite sex as something completely different. Boys often grow up thinking that if they are not strong, aggressive and competitive there is something wrong with them. Girls seem to feel they have to strive constantly to be pretty, dainty, and passive.

At school this treatment continues. Boys are often given more encouragement to do well at school as it is felt by many to be more important for them – this means that girls sometimes lose interest and do not think highly enough of their abilities. But look around your group: the girls are very much on a par with boys in terms of intelligence and ability to cope with work at school or college. Why, therefore, are girls frequently so dismissive about qualifications and future careers? Why do they often fail to fulfil their true potential?

Limiting ourselves in terms of careers and options is a problem which faces both sexes. There is surely nothing wrong in anybody wanting to work with young children or with cars and machinery, whether they be male or female. Yet many people think it odd for a girl to have an ambition to mend cars, or a boy to mind children. This kind of attitude instantly limits what are possible or probable choices in our lives. We all need to be constantly aware of the expectations of society and the pressures put upon us because of our sex. We need to be asking ourselves, 'Am I doing this, or thinking this way, because I want to, or because that is what is expected of a girl or boy?'

Thinking of ourselves in terms of 'male' or 'female' rather than a 'person' or 'human being' limits our choices in life. It also colours our attitudes to ourselves and the way others perceive us.

Amanda, the main character in *S.W.A.L.K*, is in her young teens. At this stage we are often encouraged to be more independent but are still being told what to do. It can be a difficult and confusing time for both the teenager and the parents. Amanda, like most of us, is striving to be 'acceptable' and 'normal', but it is not clear what this means. Is it the image portrayed in the teenage 'love' magazines? Is conformity always the best way, or should we be encouraged to develop our individuality? If we do want to be seen as individuals, how do we achieve this without being viewed as 'odd'?

Much of the world around us seems to be saying that we are not good enough – we should be better-looking, thinner, better-dressed, richer, more attractive to the opposite sex. This causes a feeling of discontent, instead of satisfaction and happiness with the way we are.

What we think of ourselves, and how we value everybody as individuals is important. These ideas and questions are raised and explored in some depth in *S.W.A.L.K*.

Amanda's problems at school, with friends, with family, and with boyfriends, are dilemmas many of us still experience growing up in our society.

Linda Buckle

'The Seduction'

(A clumsy poem of teenage angst!!!)

After the party, early Sunday morning,
He led her to the quiet bricks of Birkenhead docks.
Far past the silver stream of traffic through the city.
Far from the blind windows of the tower blocks.

He sat down in the darkness, leather jacket creaking madly.
He spat into the river, fumbled in a bag.
He handed her the vodka, and she knocked it back like water,
She giggled, drunk and nervous, and he muttered 'little slag'.

She had met him at the party, and he'd danced with her all night.
He'd told her about football; Sammy Lee and Ian Rush.
She had nodded, quite enchanted, and her eyes were wide and bright
As he enthused about the Milk Cup, and the next McGuigan fight.

As he brought her more drinks, so she fell in love
With his eyes as blue as iodine,
With the fingers that stroked her neck and her thighs
And the kisses that tasted of nicotine.

Then: 'I'll take you to the river where I spend the afternoons,
When I should be at school, or eating me dinner.
Where I go, by myself, with me dad's magazines
And a bag filled with shimmering, sweet paint thinner.'

So she followed him there, all high white shoes,
All wide blue eyes, and bottles of vodka.
And sat in the dark, her head rolling forward
Towards the frightening scum on the water.

And talked about school, in a disjointed way:
About O-levels she'd be sitting in June.
She chattered on, and stared at the water,
The Mersey, green as a septic wound.

Then, when he swiftly contrived to kiss her
His kiss was scented by Listerine
And she stifled a giggle, reminded of numerous
Stories from teenage magazines . . .

When she discovered she was three months gone
She sobbed in the cool, locked darkness of her room
And she ripped up all her *My Guy* and her *Jackie* photo-comics
Until they were just bright paper, like confetti, strewn

On the carpet. And on that day, she broke the heels
Of her high white shoes (as she flung them at the wall).
And realised, for once, that she was truly truly frightened
But more than that, cheated by the promise of it all.

For where, now, was the summer of her sixteenth year;
Full of glitzy fashion features, and stories of romance?
Where a stranger could lead you to bright new worlds,
And how would you know, if you never took a chance?

Full of glossy horoscopes and glamour with a stammer;
Full of fresh fruit diets – how did she feel betrayed? –
Now, with a softly rounded belly, she was sickened every morning
By stupid stupid promises, only tacitly made.

Where were the glossy photographs of summer,
Day trips to Blackpool, jumping all the rides?
And where, now, were the pink smiling faces in the picture:
Three girls paddling in the grey and frothy tide?

So she cried that she had missed all the innocence around her
And all the parties where you meet the boy next door,
Where you walk hand in hand, in an acne'd wonderland,
With a glass of lager-shandy, on a carpeted floor.

But, then again, better to be smoking scented drugs
Or festering, invisibly, unemployed.
Better to destroy your life in modern, man-made ways
Than to fall into this despicable, feminine void.

Better to starve yourself, like a sick, precocious child
Than to walk through town with a belly huge and ripe.
And better, now, to turn away, move away, fade away,
Than to have the neighbours whisper that 'you always looked the type'.

Eileen McAuley, 17

*Winner of the Young Observer
National Children's Poetry Competition*

Credits

S.W.A.L.K. was first transmitted on ITV in Britain on 12 April 1983. Given below are the credits and cast for this Thames Television production.

Casting Director	Keith Andrews
Music	Woolly Wolstenholme
	David Rhol
Film Cameraman	Alan Jonas
Film Recordist	George Thomas
Film Editor	Dan Carter
Film Dubbing	Terry Hill
Studio Cameras	Chas Watts
Studio Sound	Richard Churchill
	Peter Ball
Lighting	Allen Harradine
Studio Supervisor	Bruce Englefield
Vision Mixer	Martin Perrett
Vision Control	Bill Marley
	Allan James
VTR Editors	Colin Bocking
	Roger Holmes
Location Supervisor	Eric Pavitt
Floor Manager	Fizz Waters
Animated Camera	Peter Goodwin
Photo Stills	Gerald Sunderland
Costume	Marcia Stanton
Make-up	Ann Briggs
Stage Manager	Nigel J. Wilson
Production Assistant	Valerie Farron
Graphics Designer	Alex Forbes
Designer	David Richens
Executive Producer	Pamela Lonsdale
Producer	Sheila Kinany
Director	Richard Bramall
Written by	Paula Milne

Cast

Amanda	Nicola Cowper
Katherine	Gerry Cowper
June	Shirley Stelfox
Frank	Davyd Harries
Polly	Katy Newell
Michael	Russell Lewis
Terry	Glyn Grimstead
Gary	Marcus D'Amico
Hilary	Sandra Hall
Patti	Prunella Scales
Boy on bus	Craig Stokes
Fifth Formers	Debbie Killingback
	Astra Sheridan
	Heather Taylor
Jo	Maxine Gordon
Miss Sullivan	Frances Jeater
Girl	Frances Ruffelle
Newsreader	Philip Elsmore
Ross	Ian Seers
Dommy	Steven Woodcock
Mick	Wayne Norman
Vicar	Norman Henry
Registrar	Frank Ellis
Factory girls	Cindy Day
	Johanna Hargreaves
	Sallyanne Law
Women in clinic	Sharon Maiden
	Christina Schofield
Sister	Rosemary Williams
Woman in office	Sheila Dunn
Careers officer	P.J. Davidson
Nurse	Yvonne Gidden

S.W.A.L.K.

EPISODE ONE

'Introducing Amanda'

Synopsis

Amanda is thirteen years old. Her head is full of daydreams, fuelled by her daily diet of romantic teenage magazines. But at home there is only secrecy and silence surrounding her elder sister Katherine; a stark contrast to the simplistic, rosy world of her soap-opera magazine.

When Amanda's questions go unanswered, she turns to Patti, agony aunt and problem page pundit, who has an answer for everything – if you're young and gullible enough to believe her . . .

1 Exterior. School. Day. 1

A modern glass and concrete slab of a school. Deserted playing fields and playgrounds. Perhaps, distantly, the indistinct sound of piano scales, a telephone ringing, a chorus of voices all repeating German verbs . . .

Sounds suggesting the routine school life enclosed within these stark walls.

Another sound builds, obliterating the others. It is a rustling sound, like dry leaves in a wind . . .

Cut to:

A discarded magazine in the empty playground. The rustling sound is its pages, trembling and fluttering in the breeze.

It is a teenage girls' magazine, such as *Jackie*, *My Guy*, or *Oh Boy*.

It is called LOVE LIFE.

As the breeze nudges the pages over we catch brief glimpses of the contents . . .

1A   Standard Magazine Interior Montage.   1A

Comic strips of leggy, long-haired girls with shiny lips embracing handsome boys . . . Photo-strip soap operas depicting similar narratives . . . Problem Pages and pop stars . . . All images suggesting colour and glamour.

A soft-centred oasis in the otherwise grey and unyielding landscape of school.

And now sounds endorse this impression; whispering at first, but building and merging into a confused crescendo.

> 1ST VOICE   Tacky, dry skin? Plagued by spots and pimples?
> Let Clearagel melt those unsightly blemishes
> away . . .

As the wind teases the pages, a brief glimpse of a strip cartoon, a girl kissing a man.

> 2ND VOICE   Oh Jake . . . if you knew how I'd waited for
> this moment . . . !

Now, a Problem Page.

> 3RD VOICE   . . . discovered my boyfriend was two-timing
> me and ever since then I just can't seem to
> shake off this depression . . .

Another masculine voice chimes in.

4TH VOICE   She was only the Girl-Next-Door, until he
                decided to move in on her . . . !

And yet another.

5TH VOICE   This simple questionnaire . . . One: does your
                fella keep you waiting for dates? Two: does
                your fella know you mean no when you say it?
                Three: does your fella . . .

Still holding on the fluttering pages of the magazine, allow the
sounds to build before abruptly cutting to silence.

Superimpose the episode title, cartoon-like, in a speech
bubble.

1B   Sub-title   1B

Bring up the episode title:

Episode One, Introducing Amanda.

Cut to:

2   Int. School corridor. Day.   2

From the relative tranquility of the previous scene, a sudden
rush and gush of noisy energy.

Feet, stamping, hurtling, hustling down the corridor. Locker
doors banging closed.

Swing doors bursting open, a tide of babbling screaming kids
swarming through. Their voices raggedly ricocheting off the
walls and polished floors.

It's the end of another day.

A tiled, graffiti-scarred cloakroom. The battered doors of cubicles line one side. Bubonic-looking sinks the other. Out of view (OOV), the sounds of the school, noisily disgorging.

We open on the graffiti itself, allowing it literally to fill the screen. Eons of scrawlings with felt pen, lipstick and nail files. A testament of youth you might say.

We allow the camera to rove idly over such literary endeavours as: Sally is a Slag, Guy Loves Linda, Vice is Nice but Incest is Best, Barry for me, I hate soul, SH rates LM.

During this, voices, OOV.

Cut to:

Three or so fifth-year girls, aged about fifteen to sixteen, preening in front of the mirror, combing hair and applying lip gloss.

Their only token to school uniform is perhaps a blazer, or the school badge, stuck onto a sports bag.

The shelf beneath the mirror is chock-a-block with bulging make-up kits, hairbrushes and hair sprays.

They converse in disconnected half-sentences, clearly familiar with each others thoughts, in a world very much of their own.

One of the girls is holding another's hair off her neck, while applying make-up to camouflage a love-bite.

Perhaps it is the way it's shot, or the singular confidence the girls seem to exude, but they should strike us as being old, rather than young, self-assured and disconcertingly together.

We pick them up mid-dialogue, addressing their reflections as much as each other.

     1ST GIRL . . . she told me she chucked him . . .

2ND GIRL   Chucked him?

3RD GIRL   She had to say something, didn't she?

All this while eyes squint to receive mascara, and combs deftly comb.

3RD GIRL   She told Trisha he stood her up.

2ND GIRL   Trisha?

1ST GIRL   When?

3RD GIRL   Last week.

1ST GIRL   Not what she told us.

3RD GIRL   What Trisha said.

2ND GIRL   Well she told me *she* chucked *him*.

3RD GIRL   Hmm.

Lips are contemplatively smacked as they digest this last information.

We cut to see a girl watching them. This is AMANDA.

AMANDA is thirteen years old, the so-called awkward age. Still a child to her parents, an adult to herself, an outlaw to the world she is covertly observing now.

Now we understand why the Fifth Formers seemed more mature than their years. It is because the whole scene is shot and played from Amanda's viewpoint.

As the FIFTH FORMERS prattle on, she watches.

1ST GIRL   Mind you, Trisha would.

2ND GIRL   Would what?

1ST GIRL   Say that. She went with him herself, didn't she?

2ND GIRL   Trisha?

1ST GIRL   Last term.

3RD GIRL   Only the once though.

1ST GIRL	Three weeks she told me.
3RD GIRL	Three weeks!
2ND GIRL	I thought he went with Debby last term?
1ST GIRL	(*Derisively*) That was *Garry*.
2ND GIRL	O–o–o–h.

During all this, another thirteen year-old emerges from the cubicles. This is POLLY, best friend of AMANDA.

Whereas AMANDA is lower middle class, POLLY is definitely middle, with all the manifest confidence that can go with it.

It is a paradoxical relationship of opposites, in that AMANDA seems to rely on POLLY's assurance, as if hoping that some of it might somehow rub off on her.

POLLY for her part, gets her assurance from AMANDA's very lack of it. In short they have an instinctive, unspoken mutual need for each other. Both unconsciously complimenting the other's deficiencies.

As she washes her hands, POLLY too listens to the fifth-year prattle. But unlike AMANDA, her expression is more cynical, more critical.

The Fifth Formers' endeavours with make-up and mirror are now complete. Make-up kits are zipped up. Final checks are made on painted lips and faces.

1ST GIRL	Right . . . my place again or . . . ?
3RD GIRL	I thought we were going for a coffee.
2ND GIRL	He won't be there . . . he never is on Thursdays.
3RD GIRL	We can try, can't we.
2ND GIRL	It's a waste of time – he works late Thursdays doesn't he?
3RD GIRL	Says who?

The latter part of this is lost to us, as their voices ebb and recede.

> POLLY Good riddance.
> (*She pulls a face in the mirror, pouting her lips as they did*) 'And *he* said to me that *she* said to her, that *I* said to him . . . '
> (*To Amanda*) What's that?

AMANDA is examining a plastic wand thing, a holder containing mascara. They look at it with idle curiosity.

> AMANDA It's practically new.

> POLLY More fool them.

AMANDA puts an experimental dab on her eyes.

> POLLY Yuk, You don't know where it's been. (*As she moves*) Are you coming or what?

Hastily AMANDA replaces the mascara and follows her.

We hold on the discarded mascara.

Cut to:

---

4 Int. Cosmetics Factory. Day.   4

An army of hundreds of identical mascaras jostling together on a conveyor belt. We pull out to reveal we are inside a cosmetics factory.

Sullen-faced, bored-looking girls in caps and overalls are checking the mascaras as they go by.

Beyond, we can see the blur of the factory. More uniformed girls and conveyor belts. A loud speaker blasting out distorted pop music.

Now a few snatched shots of face creams squirting unappetisingly into containers . . . Face powder being compressed in compacts by machines . . . hair cream belching into tubes . . .

The vanity industry, not at its best perhaps, but as it really is.

Now we see one girl in particular. As we'll later discover, this is KATHERINE, sister of AMANDA.

Like the others, she wears an overall. Like the others, she is bone-achingly, painfully bored. One eye on the clock, one on the job in hand.

Pull out to isolate her on the noisy clamouring shop floor.

Cut to:

5   Ext. School Gates. Day.   5

POLLY and AMANDA, approaching the school gates, where a small cluster of sixth-year girls are gathered.

They are dispensing sheets of paper and brandishing a placard which boldly states: 'EQUAL RIGHTS MEANS EQUAL EDUCATION'.

Passing boys cat call derisively. Even the younger girls don't seem interested, and hasten by on their way.

>   AMANDA What's going on?

>   POLLY Search me. Looks like some kind of protest.
>   Come on.

They duck down slightly, as they walk swiftly by, taking advantage of some boys trying to snatch at the wads of papers held by the Sixth Formers, which provides a momentary distraction . . .

But too late, a Sixth Former has spotted them. She is dressed like a punk. A maverick by nature, restless, wayward and impulsive. Her name is HILARY.

>   HILARY Hey . . . !

>   POLLY Run for it!

Giggling and clutching their bags, POLLY and AMANDA start to hot foot it away.

> HILARY Oy, you two . . . !
>
>> (*But AMANDA and POLLY run obliviously on*) Oh very funny! Very cute!

But they turn a corner and are lost to her.

Cut to:

6 Int. Top of Bus. Day.   6

A dense fog of cigarette smoke. A cassette recorder blaring out rock music.

A gang of boys, aged around fourteen to fifteen, sit in the back seats, legs straddled over seats in front, shouting together and arguing. They are lobbing paper pellets and matchsticks at the girls, sitting further up the bus.

Pick out POLLY and AMANDA, running up the steps and slumping into a seat.

They spot the congregation of boys and exchange a knowing look.

A passing pellet hits AMANDA on the cheek.

> AMANDA Creeps.

POLLY turns to address the BOYS.

> POLLY Why don't you just crawl back into your holes?
>
> BOY That the best you can do, is it?
>
> AMANDA Ignore them.
>
> POLLY Louts. All of them.
>
> BOY Who are you calling a lout?
>
> POLLY You . . .

AMANDA   So lay off.

BOY   Or what?

POLLY and AMANDA pointedly turn their backs as the boys continue to snigger and laugh behind them.

And we see another boy, GARY, sitting a little distance away from the others. Part of the group, yet somehow isolated from them.

GARY is less scruffy than the others, less rowdy in demeanour and manner. He sits, a book open on his lap, watching POLLY and AMANDA, as if somehow, despite himself, intrigued by them . . .

We return to AMANDA and POLLY. The former catches sight of HILARY, still holding her placard of Equal Rights, mounting the steps of the bus.

AMANDA   Uh-oh!

POLLY   Now what?

AMANDA grimaces and gestures towards HILARY who is approaching them.

POLLY   Pretend you're reading.

They snatch out a magazine and bury their heads in it. But HILARY is wise to such tactics.

HILARY   I suppose you thought that was funny. (*They stare innocently at her*) Running off like that.

POLLY   Running off? (*To Amanda*) Did we run off?

AMANDA giggles.

AMANDA   I don't know. Did we?
HILARY   We're not doing this for the fun of it you know. It's for you as much as us.

POLLY   (*Sweetly*) Doing what?

AMANDA   (*Equally sweetly*) Exactly?

HILARY is not impressed.

HILARY   Quite a little comedy act, aren't we?

POLLY   We like to think so.

HILARY   We want to persuade the school to let us take
the same classes as the boys. Metalwork and
woodwork and that sort of thing.

AMANDA   Why?

HILARY   Why?! Why should we be fobbed off with
domestic science or needlework while they do
all the interesting things? It should be our
choice what subjects we take, not the school's!

POLLY   Who wants to do metalwork?

AMANDA   Or woodwork?

POLLY   Definitely not woodwork.

HILARY regards them again, much as one might regard a lost cause.

HILARY   It's the principle isn't it? We should be allowed
the same chances as the boys . . . same classes,
same career opportunities, same everything.
(*She gives a sheet of paper to POLLY*) You'll be the
ones to lose out if you don't join us.

*And she rises, with her placard, to join her peers at the front of the
bus. AMANDA looks over POLLY's shoulder at the bit of paper.*

AMANDA   What does it say?

POLLY   (*Reading*) 'We believe that girls are equal to
boys and that this should be reflected in the
educational system. We also believe that . . . '

*But her discourse is interrupted by another pellet from the boys at
the rear of the bus.*

POLLY   Right . . . That's it. That – is – it!

Rolling up the sheet of paper, POLLY hurls it at the BOYS defiantly. Both paper and its message are irrevocably lost.

7   Int. Cosmetics Factory. Day.   7

KATHERINE, at her post again.

Her eyes on her watch which grudgingly inches to four o'clock.

The end-of-shift bell rings, she switches off the machine she is operating, and thankfully departs.

8   Ext. Cosmetics Factory. Day.   8

A swarm of GIRLS exit through the factory gates. They are reminiscent of the school children leaving school. Except these are adults, but none the less grateful it's the end of another day.

We pick out KATHERINE amongst them. She is waving to someone. A boy on a motor cycle. This is TERRY. He is clad in leather, and his face is obscured by a crash helmet and visor.

As he waves back to her, cut to:

9   Ext. Bus. Day.   9

AMANDA'S FACE, framed in an upper window of the bus.

She is also waving, and our impression should be, at least momentarily, that it is the boy on the motor bike she is waving at . . .

But we cut, to see it is actually POLLY, briefly waving back to her, before trudging off down the road.

Cut to:

The rowdy BOYS, still in the back of the bus.

AMANDA, now alone and slightly apprehensive of that fact, delves into her bag, and brings out a copy of LOVE LIFE.

A brief shot of GARY, who was watching earlier, covertly watching her, as he too reads.

The BOYS at the back continue to lob pellets and cigarette ends at her.

> BOY   Oy, mousie! . . . where's your friend?

AMANDA makes a great play out of concentrating on her magazine.

It is open on the Problem Page, called 'Patti's Problem Page'. We shoot it, as from Amanda's viewpoint. Letters from love-lorn, love-torn teenage girls.

And in the top right hand corner, a circle, containing a portrait photograph of a woman, cropped hair, motherly smile, beaming brightly at us. This is PATTI.

As the cat calls and shouts from the boys continue, OOV, she speaks:

> PATTI   Boy problems? Don't let them get you down, girls. Write to Patti's Problem Page . . . not so much a shoulder to cry on, as a friend to lean on . . . !

AMANDA'S FACE, almost dreamy.

She looks wistfully out of the window.

Hold on AMANDA'S FACE and bring up her voice, OOV.

> AMANDA (*Voice over [VO]*) Dear Patti, there must be something wrong with me because I seem to find most boys really childish and stupid . . . All except Terry that is. (*She glances down at the magazine and turns a page. A true-to-life soap opera is depicted there. VO cont.*) Terry's really different . . .

A stillness settles over everything. The noise of the boys behind her fades away.

The fog of cigarette smoke suddenly seems more like a romantic haze.

10A   Fantasy Sequence. Bus.   10A

The image of AMANDA now dissipates into a fantasy photo effect of her, reminiscent of the true-to-life photo strips that she reads.

She looks up to see a shadow looming over her.

We see a BOY of around nineteen or twenty standing there. Dressed in leather, a seductive smile creasing his handsome face.

This is TERRY, boy of her waking and sleeping dreams. And he has eyes only for her. A thought bubble appears over her head.

AMANDA (Oh Terry . . .)

Now a speech bubble is over his.

TERRY (Hi . . . Mind if I join you?)

A look of ecstasy on her face, accompanied by another thought bubble.

AMANDA 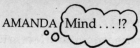 Mind . . . !?

Cut to:

A shot of AMANDA and TERRY seated side by side in the bus.
The same romantic haze surrounding them. Her, gazing up
at him.
A speech bubble appears over his head.

TERRY | Thought maybe those creeps were giving you
some trouble.

Another bubble over hers.

AMANDA (Nothing you can't handle, Terry.)

Cut to:

11 Fantasy Sequence cont. Ext. Amanda's   11
House.

Still using caricature photographic effects we see TERRY and
AMANDA walking hand in hand down the street.
Somehow they contrive to continue gazing into each others
eyes without falling flat on their faces.

AMANDA | They can't help acting like kids I suppose . . .
I used to think that's how you thought of me.
As just a kid.

TERRY | Once perhaps. I just never looked closely
before. I must have been blind.

AMANDA (Oh Terry . . . !

They are now outside her house. A semi-detached, 1930s pebble dash, bow-windowed house, surrounded by other identical ones.

AMANDA is dreamily smiling at TERRY. A shot of her, a misty look in her eyes. As she watches him leave, the photographic effects dissipate back into live action once more. We are back into reality and real time.

11A   Ext. Amanda's House. Day.   11A

AMANDA is entering her house.

12   Int. Amanda's House. Day.   12

AMANDA enters, and starts to unbutton her anorak.

As she does so, the sound of raised voices alerts her. Voices raised in anger, if not acrimony. A storm is obviously brewing.

AMANDA'S
   MOTHER   (*VO*) What do you mean encourage her! When
               have I ever encouraged her? When!

AMANDA'S
   FATHER   (*VO*) You've never *dis*couraged her have you?
               Never told her she could do better for herself!

AMANDA *moves to listen outside the kitchen door.*

AMANDA'S
   MOTHER   (*VO*) and you have I suppose? My God, you
               haven't spoken to that girl for months!

AMANDA'S
   FATHER   (*VO*) You're her mother. It's a mother's job to
               tell her daughter these things . . .

AMANDA'S

    MOTHER (*VO*) Very handy! Very convenient! Now it's all
        my fault!

During this, AMANDA hovers uncertainly. Her brother
MICHAEL comes down the hall stairs. He is sixteen. Taciturn,
monosyllabic.

He is heading for the front door.

    AMANDA (*A hissed whisper*) What's going on?

    MICHAEL You'll find out.

He goes, banging the front door after him. AMANDA looks
apprehensively at the kitchen.

13   Int. Amanda's Kitchen. Day. Studio.   13

Open on AMANDA'S MOTHER, a woman in her early middle
age. Once attractive, now careworn, anxious.

She is dishevelled and distressed, clattering with dishes and
plates in an attempt to distract herself. Her name is JUNE.

Her husband FRANK is pacing the floor, more angry than
upset.

Like her, he is in his early middle age, a mild-mannered man
usually. A man of hobbies rather than action, but galvanised
now by anger and disappointment. He is wearing a modest
suit, as if for work. He is a salesman.

We should feel that their anger is not really directed at each
other, but rather at themselves. As if whatever it is that has
happened is somehow an accusation, a personal reproach of
their failure . . .

As they talk AMANDA enters, unseen.

    FRANK Dragging me home from work like that mid
           afternoon . . . what the hell do you expect me
           to do?

JUNE (*Simply*) When they rang I just thought you should be here.

FRANK To do what?

JUNE We have to talk to her, don't we?

FRANK Talk! It's a pity she didn't think of that, isn't it?

He breaks off, catching sight of AMANDA.

FRANK and JUNE exchange a look.

The tension between them seems, inexplicably, to be replaced by embarrassment.

FRANK Go to your room, Amanda.

AMANDA looks from him to her mother.

AMANDA Why? What's happened?

JUNE Do as your father says, Amanda, please.

AMANDA But . . .

JUNE Just do as he says!

Reluctantly AMANDA opens the door. But turns back.

AMANDA What about my tea?

This innocent request seems to be the last straw for FRANK. Angrily he marches over to her, grabbing her by the shoulders.

FRANK Will–you–just–do–as–you're–told!

And unceremoniously he shoves her out of the room.

14 Int. Amanda's Hall. Day. Studio.   14

AMANDA's face, as her FATHER bustles her roughly out of the kitchen and slams the door on her. Her expression hurt and bewildered, as much as angry.
Their voices continue, OOV.

> JUNE (*VO*) Taking it out on the rest of us isn't going to help is it?

> FRANK (*VO*) Don't go on, woman!

Then, the unmistakable sound of JUNE sobbing.

> FRANK And don't start that . . . it doesn't help either, does it?

AMANDA has apparently heard enough. She runs up the stairs to her room.

15   Int. Amanda's Bedroom. Day. Studio.   15

The walls adorned with pop stars. Very much a girl's bedroom, the dressing table littered with jars of cold cream. Clothes hanging off hangers on picture rails and wardrobe doors.

There are two beds in the room. As we'll discover, AMANDA shares it with KATHERINE.

There is a record player in one corner, and stacked in piles by one of the beds, more 'love-life'-type teenage magazines.

AMANDA runs into the room, hurls herself onto her bed. Anger and resentment now beginning to replace her earlier bewilderment.

As she lies there, head buried in pillow, a cartoon-style circle appears in the top right of frame.

PATTI'S FACE, framed within it. She smiles at AMANDA, all sugary sympathy.

> PATTI That draggy generation gap again, right? Still treating you like a kid? I don't know, they never learn do they? . . . Still, you're luckier than some. At least you've someone to turn to. Someone pretty special at that.

AMANDA raises her head from the pillow. Her eyes widen. Once more live action is replaced by the photographic effects.

15A   Fantasy. Amanda's Bedroom. Day. Int.   15A

TERRY is seated on a chair by the dressing table. He smiles his irresistible smile.

A speech bubble appears over his head.

TERRY (Hi . . .)

AMANDA'S FACE. That misty look again.

TERRY (Heard you were having some aggro . . . Can't have that, can we?)

He holds out a hand to her.

TERRY (Wanta tell me about it?)

Hesitantly she rises, stretching out her hand to his. Their fingertips are almost touching when the sound of the front door banging OOV, fractures and splinters into the fantasy.

AMANDA halts, her eyes moving towards her bedroom window. As she does so the fantasy photo effect once again dissolves into live action.

15B   Amanda's Bedroom. Day. Int. Studio.   15B

We're back into real time again.

Cut to:

KATHERINE is in the hall, pulling off her coat.

As she does so, AMANDA races down the stairs.

> AMANDA Kath, there's something going on . . . with
> Mum and Dad . . . I . . .

Her voice trails off.

The front door is opening, the leather-clad BOY on the motor
bike we saw earlier enters. He still wears his crash helmet
and visor, so that his features are obscured from us.

As AMANDA watches, open-mouthed, he wrenches off his
crash helmet.

Is it that the speed of the action has imperceptibly slowed
down, or does his blonde hair seem to float and cascade as he
shakes it loose of the crash helmet?

Be that as it may, one thing is clear: the boy standing in front
of us and the open-mouthed AMANDA is none other than
TERRY . . .

He glances at her casually, as he moves towards KATHERINE.

> TERRY Hi, kid.

As AMANDA watches, he sets down the crash helmet, and
glances at himself in the hall mirror.

As TERRY does so, the kitchen door opens, and AMANDA's
FATHER emerges.

He pulls up, on seeing KATHERINE and TERRY.

> KATHERINE Hello, Dad.

> FRANK I want a word with you.

KATHERINE and TERRY exchange a glance as they walk
towards the kitchen. The door is closed behind them.

AMANDA'S FACE, more than just excluded.

17   Ext. Residential Street. Day. Film 7 a.m.   17

A street of semi-detached houses, still silent and asleep.

AMANDA is criss-crossing the street, delivering newspapers.
Maybe the drone of a milk float nearby. We let her go about
her business for a while before cutting to a closer shot.

AMANDA is just coming out from a front gate, when
something arrests her attention. A WOMAN, a BABY in her
arms, stands in front of the neighbouring house. She is
kissing her HUSBAND goodbye. Just a routine, daily activity,
but it none the less causes AMANDA to pause. And ponder.

As the WOMAN waves to her HUSBAND and moves back to
her front door, the image becomes animated so that
eventually the reality of the picture is lost and we are left
once again with a cartoon, caricature-type animation,
complete with speech bubbles and voice over.

Cut to:

18   Fantasy Sequence. Int. Cartoon Woman's   18
House. Day.

The WOMAN is entering her house, BABY in arms.

The few lines in the drawing suggest an impression of chintz
and a 'Home Sweet Home' sign.

As the WOMAN moves to the window, in order to wave her
HUSBAND goodbye once again, the VOICE OVER starts.

A confidential masculine, mid-atlantic drawl.

VOICE OVER Judy knows the importance of freshness. And
not just keeping her house fresh and hygenic
either.

JUDY we now see, bears a remarkable resemblance to AMANDA.

VOICE OVER (*Cont.*) Judy knows the importance of personal freshness. But she nearly had to learn the hard way.

The picture ripples and shimmers. We are back in time, at a disco.

JUDY is with a FRIEND. Both girls are dressed in shiny trousers with shiny lips to match.

A BOY is approaching them.

A speech bubble appears over JUDY's head:

JUDY (Hey, he's coming over . . .)

He pauses by them.

BOY (Wanta dance?)

He and JUDY move to the dance floor. By now we should have twigged that the boy is in fact Judy's husband of the future.

They start to dance. A thought bubble appears over JUDY's head:

JUDY (Mmm. He's nice. I hope he'll ask to see me again.)

But after the dance is over the BOY just walks off. Shot of JUDY'S FACE.

JUDY (Charming!)

On the way home, JUDY confides in her FRIEND.

JUDY 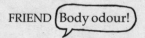 What did I do wrong? I just don't understand it . . .

Her FRIEND tells her some home truths.

FRIEND 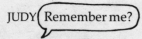 Body odour!

VOICE OVER So on her friend's advice she bought herself a can of FRAGRANCE. The next Saturday-night disco was a different story . . .

JUDY walks up to the BOY:

JUDY Remember me?

They start to dance and kiss.

VOICE OVER Two years later, Judy still uses FRAGRANCE . . . because she knows it's not just the way to get your man – but to keep him.

JUNE (*OOV*) Amanda?

Cut to:

19 Int. Amanda's kitchen. Day. Studio.   19

The whole family seated around the breakfast table.

FRANK is reading a tabloid newspaper. MICHAEL a motor-bike magazine. KATHERINE is simply eating pensively. AMANDA is absorbed in a comic strip in her teenage magazine. JUNE is addressing her from the sink.

JUNE Amanda?

AMANDA rouses from her reverie.

Everybody is avoiding catching the other person's eye. KATHERINE is apparently concentrating on eating, JUNE on serving breakfast, FRANK and MICHAEL on their reading matter.

But it all camouflages something else. Something unacknowledged beneath the surface.

> JUNE Do you have to read that at table? I don't know, you seem to spend all your time either day dreaming or with your head stuck in one of those things.

> AMANDA They're reading.

> MICHAEL Not that rubbish I'm not. No way.

> AMANDA It is not rubbish.

FRANK pulls the magazine over and glances at it briefly.

> FRANK Romantic clap trap . . . filling your mind with a load of pipe dreams . . . if you're going to bring stuff home from that newsagent, bring a decent paper, find out what's going on in the world.

> KATHERINE Leave her alone.

FRANK regards her a moment.

> FRANK Yes, well you're the expert, aren't you? Precious good they did you.

Abruptly KATHERINE leaves the table, banging the door after her.

AMANDA'S FACE, looking from parent to parent. No clue in their faces . . .

20   Int. Amanda's Bedroom. Day. Studio.   20

AMANDA zipping up her school bag, ready for school. She hastily pulls the cover over her unmade bed and exits.

21   Int. Amanda's Hall. Upstairs. Studio. Day.   21

AMANDA, about to go downstairs. The sound of voices alerts her. She moves to a bedroom door, in fact her parents', and pauses outside it, listening.

AMANDA'S FACE trying to fathom this.

> JUNE (*OOV*) He's just . . . disappointed. He had such high hopes for you all. There's Michael, wanting to leave school with no exams and no job . . . Amanda's head full of nothing but boys and pop stars. And now you. Why didn't you tell us?

> KATHERINE (*VO*) I was going to tell you, of course I was . . . how was I to know Terry'd tell his parents first? You talk like my life's over! Like it's the end of everything! I thought it was supposed to be the beginning.

> JUNE Katherine, you are just being totally unrealistic.

> KATHERINE I'm not . . .

AMANDA'S FACE still perplexed, and faintly apprehensive.

22   Int. Girls Toilet. School. Day.   22

The graffiti-scarred walls again.

AMANDA, idly, sullenly, examining her reflection in the mirror. POLLY is in one of the loos, which doesn't inhibit their conversation.

POLLY (*OOV*) Maybe she just wants to jack in her job.

AMANDA She hates her job. She says it bores her stupid.
I just don't see why everyone else is let in on it
but me . . . Even Michael knows but won't say
anything.

POLLY You know what they say. Little sisters are
always the last to know.

Shot of AMANDA'S FACE.

23 Int. Sixth-Form Common Room. Day. 23 Studio.

More informal than the usual classroom. Desks and chairs
pushed to one side. A dozen or so PUPILS from all years,
mostly girls, scattered around on the floor, sitting on
cupboards. On the walls are posters with slogans about equal
rights in education.

Generally, the atmosphere is rowdy. Some of the GIRLS are
looking at magazines, others trying on make-up, much
giggling and mucking about.

HILARY moves to the front, and tries to address them.

HILARY OK then, settle down. (*The girls continue with
their antics*) I said settle down! (*Still the noise
continues*) Look, if you're not going to listen –
it's pretty bloody pointless isn't it?

Still the noise prevails. We hold on HILARY'S FACE. Her
anger and frustration mounting.

The noise eventually stops.

HILARY What it all boils down to is this. We believe that
        girls just aren't getting a fair crack at some
        subjects. Like technical drawing and
        engineering and so on. Now we've gone
        through the school council and asked for
        something to be done, and all we get is
        platitudes and soft soap. So we have to set
        about a way of getting the school curriculum
        altered ourselves.

A shot of the PUPILS now, listening, but idly for the most
part, as if her words don't really strike much of a chord.

We see the BOY once again, covertly flicking his eyes in the
direction of AMANDA.

HILARY So the first thing to do, (*acidly*) for those of you
        who haven't nodded off, is talk to people . . .
        your families . . . friends . . . anyone who
        might support us and write to the school.

We hold now on AMANDA. The disc appears right of frame,
with PATTI'S FACE within it.

She is whispering to AMANDA.

PATTI Oh Amanda . . . ?

HILARY Then we want you to sign this petition . . .
        boys as well as girls . . . to show how deep the
        feeling is.

PATTI Hey, Amanda!

PATTI finally succeeds in getting Amanda's attention.

PATTI All this talk about options . . . where will it get
       you? I know you're down about Terry being
       Katherine's, but there are plenty more where
       he came from, right?

38

HILARY'S VOICE continues during this.

> HILARY (*OOV*) If you read it you'll see we're not only
> after stating our demands, but setting up a
> meeting with the teachers to see if and how we
> can get them realised.

> PATTI (*Overriding this*) Look around you, there's him
> for a start.

She nods towards the BOY, sitting near them. The same boy
we saw on the bus.

AMANDA follows her glance.

> PATTI Sure, he's new to the school, but that just gives
> you a head start . . . Forget all this nonsense
> and concentrate on what's important . . . And
> he could be important if you'd give him the
> chance.

AMANDA looks curiously at the BOY. PATTI, smiling, her job
completed, fades away.

And HILARY continues, oblivious and ignored in the
background.

24   Int. Amanda's Hall. Day. Studio.   24

AMANDA and POLLY entering through the front door.
Pulling off their anoraks and coats. We pick up POLLY, mid-
conversation.

> POLLY I thought it made a lot of sense.

> AMANDA We'll look real idiots if we get all these classes
> and then no-one wants to do them, won't we?

> POLLY But she's talking about the *principle* of it, isn't
> she?

AMANDA   That's just what it is, if you ask me . . . a load of
talk. (*Then glancing at the kitchen*) Ssshhh . . .

They move surreptitiously towards the kitchen door, which
is ajar. We can see JUNE within, talking on the telephone.

Both GIRLS pause, listening.

JUNE   Yes, well it was a surprise to us too . . . No,
Terry's mother rang us . . . I suppose boys find
it easier to tell their parents these things . . .

AMANDA shuts the door and turns to POLLY.

AMANDA   See, it's like this all the time.

25   Int. Amanda's Bedroom. Day. Studio.   25

AMANDA, POLLY and KATHERINE are listening to records in
Amanda's bedroom. JUNE enters.

JUNE   Amanda, will you give me a hand with this tea?
(*She breaks off, seeing Polly*) Oh, Polly . . .
Oh . . . (*She seems more flustered and
embarrassed than anything*) About tonight
. . . I don't want to be inhospitable but . . .
(*to Polly*) We've rather a family crisis on . . .

A pause: POLLY'S FACE.

26   Int. Amanda's Kitchen. Evening. Studio.   26

The FAMILY, assembled around the table eating. But the meal
is held in silence, save for the clatter of cutlery on plates.

Once again, we're holding on AMANDA'S FACE, viewing it
all from her stance, as she looks from her sister to brother,
and parent to parent.

The silence continues.

Cut to:

Later. AMANDA is dutifully, if sullenly, helping her mother with the supper dishes.

> JUNE No point sulking, Amanda. (*Amanda says nothing, but clatters around with pots and pans*) I said she could come another night.

> AMANDA You still haven't said why she couldn't stop tonight.

> JUNE Because your father and I . . . (*she seems about to elaborate, but changes tack*) We wouldn't be very good company. (*Amanda says nothing*) It doesn't help you kicking up a silly fuss about nothing.

> AMANDA I don't even know what the fuss is all about, do I?

FRANK enters at this point, to collect the evening paper from the table. He and JUNE exchange a tactical glance before he withdraws.

> JUNE I don't know what fuss you mean . . . (*Now it's her turn to sound casual*) Your sister's getting married, that's all.

27   Int. Amanda's Bedroom. Night. Studio.   27

AMANDA in bed, KATHERINE preparing to do the same. Pick up the dialogue as the scene opens.

> KATHERINE (*Casually*) That's all Mum said, is it? Just that we're getting married?

> AMANDA Yes.

> KATHERINE (*More to herself*) Nothing changes does it.

KATHERINE Tosses the magazine onto the pile and moves over to her bed, switching off the light as she does.

For a moment both girls lie in the semi-darkness, each preoccupied with their own thoughts.

KATHERINE I remember when I first got my period . . . a year or so younger than you . . . Mum just couldn't wait to get the explanations over with, she was that embarrassed. In fact she was in such a hurry I got it all wrong . . . I thought it was something that happened just once and that was it. Finito. A month later, bingo, it happened again. She and Dad had some people in and I was just going to bed when big discovery, there it was again. I thought I was a freak or something . . . (*Amanda's face in the darkness listening*) so I went charging downstairs in my nightie, flung open the sitting room door and said, 'Mother – it's happened again!' Didn't go down too well.

AMANDA She never told me about it at all. Not properly.

KATHERINE She didn't have to did she? She knew she had me to do it for her. (*Then, irritably*) I don't know why she can't see it.

AMANDA See what?

KATHERINE That all this . . . secrecy and stuff just makes these things worse. (*She glances at Amanda, and then props herself up, switching on the light again. It's like she's made a decision.*) Look, you didn't get it from me, OK? Let her think you just twigged it on your own.

AMANDA Twigged what?

KATHERINE (*Impatiently*) What all the aggro's been about of course.

As AMANDA stares at her:

KATHERINE I'm pregnant, aren't I?

And so saying, KATHERINE snaps off the light, and lies back in the bed.

We hold AMANDA'S FACE in the darkness. Freeze frame.

PATTI'S FACE appears in the circle, to the right of the top of frame.

This time she is addressing us, in her mock confidential way.

PATTI Will Katherine and Terry live happily ever after?
Will Amanda's secret admirer declare himself?
Will Polly and Amanda join the sixth form revolution? (*As the image of both AMANDA and PATTI fades* . . .) To be continued . . .
next week.

End of Episode One

A closer look at . . .

Teenage 'love' magazines

Amanda, like most of us, is very much influenced by the magazines she reads. 'Romantic love' magazines are very popular. How similar are they to each other in content, approach and values?

They usually contain stories about relationships with boys, advice on how to be more attractive to the opposite sex, 'problem pages' with letters (usually connected with boys and doubts about appearance), pin-ups of well-known men that girls are supposed to find attractive, and well-known women that are meant to be emulated. These magazines are always aimed at girls. Why is this? Consider what kind of magazines boys are encouraged to read.

It is worth looking at the values these 'love' magazines encourage their readers to have. Their attitude to life is simplistic. All the girls depicted in the stories and articles appear to have the same aims in life: they are obsessed by dates with boys, and their only ambition in life is marriage. This suggests that all girls are the same and want to be the same. Do you think this is true? Do most people have similar plans for their future? When you think of the life ahead of you, do you want the same things as your friends, girls and boys?

The positive values of education, careers, health, friends and family are rarely, if ever, explored in these magazines. Friendly relationships with either sex are barely touched upon. People of the opposite sex are viewed as something apart, intrinsically different – either to be 'fancied' or left alone (if you think like this you are ruling out half the population as possible friends). The stories in these magazines tend to view people of the same sex as competition in the race to get an acceptable boyfriend or girlfriend. Friends are shown to be useful only if there is no one of the opposite sex on the scene. What do you think of this way of viewing friends? Is it a way of treating others that you have seen happen, or been guilty of yourself?

Have a look at the advertisements in such magazines. What kind of products are being advertised and who are they aimed at? What tactics are they using to encourage people to buy? What role do the advertisements have in creating our attitudes? Readers are encouraged to view and judge each other in a very physical way. The way you look seems to determine your value. The more you resemble the model in the hairspray advert or the fashionable pop-star, the more it implies you are worth as a person. In what other ways should we judge the people around us?

Magazines like this encourage and advise girls on how to become what boys are supposed to like. It would be interesting to ask the boys in the group what they think of the girls and relationships portrayed in such magazines. Are they the kind of relationships you have had – or would like to experience? It is interesting to look more closely at these relationships. What do the two people involved actually say to each other? How well do they seem to know each other? Do people really talk that way?

How could such a magazine be re-organised and what could it include to make it less sexist? The magazine editors would probably say they are producing what people want – but is this true? Consider how much choice there really is on the magazine racks for young people. Are all girls destined to graduate from teenage 'love' magazines to women's magazines dealing with the home, family, and fashion?

'Happy Ever After'

Synopsis

Amanda's sister Katherine is pregnant and getting married. To Amanda, it is everything a girl can aspire to: this ideal is relentlessly re-inforced by the ever-persistent Patti, and the idyllic images of her teenage magazines.

However, this picture does not reflect Katherine's feelings. She is growing increasingly uneasy about the direction in which her life is going. But she is powerless to prevent the plans her family are making on her behalf, or acknowledge that she does not want the child she is bearing.

1   Int. Amanda's Bedroom. Day. Studio.   1

Open on AMANDA's bed, literally littered with magazines. All of them are the romantic, cartoon or photo-strip variety, depicting true-to-life soap operas . . . Boys kissing wide-eyed, frothy-haired girls . . . Symbols of broken hearts and tear drops . . . Problem Pages, beauty hints, pop stars . . .

1A   Standard Int. Magazine Montage.   1A

Opening montage. The camera almost leisurely, pans over the images, allowing them to fill the screen . . . As in Episode One, we build up the sounds, voices, huskily whispering, tenderly cajoling, sexy and persuasive. Each one, building in intensity and volume, becoming a discordant, ragged chorus, as the appropriate images continue to swim before our eyes.

Bring up the episode title:

Episode Two, Happy Ever After.

1C   Amanda's Bedroom. Day. Int. Studio.   1C

AMANDA is sitting at the dressing table, brushing her hair. From her desultory movements we can assume she is preparing for school.

Propped up on the dressing table is a framed photograph – it shows a handsome, beaming young man whom we should recognise as TERRY from Episode One.

AMANDA glances at the photograph and pauses, picking it up. Something almost wistful in her face.

The disc, containing PATTI'S FACE, appears right of frame. We become aware of muted sounds *OOV*. There is the sound of retching coming from the direction of the bathroom.

PATTI   Go on, try it on, she won't mind . . .

AMANDA hesitates a moment and then puts the photograph down. She opens a drawer and takes out a small velvet-covered box.

It contains an engagement ring.

Tentatively she takes out the ring and tries it on, extending her hand, to examine the effect.

PATTI   Well, it's a perfect fit isn't it? Perfect . . .

Hastily AMANDA pulls off the ring and replaces it, as the disc containing PATTI'S FACE evaporates.

KATHERINE enters. She is still in her nightdress and looks decidedly green about the gills. Plaintively, she lowers herself onto her bed.

AMANDA glances at her as she resumes brushing her hair.

> AMANDA It's probably a tummy bug, everyone's going down with it at school . . .

> KATHERINE I doubt many of them are eight weeks pregnant.

KATHERINE takes in AMANDA's expression. AMANDA'S FACE, slightly perplexed.

A moment of silence.

> AMANDA (*Curiously*) Can you feel anything yet?

> KATHERINE Like what?

> AMANDA You know. It. Inside.

> KATHERINE It's only about an inch long, if that. (*She reaches for a book by the bedside*) Look . . .

The book is called something like *The Joys of Motherhood*. A kind of obstetric guide through pregnancy.

KATHERINE flips through some pages until she comes to a diagram. It shows a small blobby-like drawing, supposedly the foetus at eight weeks.

AMANDA sits on the bed next to her and both GIRLS look at the drawing. Rotating the book sideways, as one might an abstract drawing, when you're trying to make some kind of sense out of it.

> AMANDA (*Faintly disappointed*) Is that it?

> KATHERINE Not much to write home about is it?

AMANDA peers at the drawing closely.

> AMANDA Are they supposed to be eyes or what?

KATHERINE   They must be. There some blurb on it
            somewhere.

KATHERINE   She starts to flick through the book again.
            AMANDA rises and continues to get ready.
            KATHERINE starts to read aloud.

KATHERINE   'At eight weeks the major organs of the foetus
            are formed. The heart is beating. The
            circulatory system is well established. The chest
            is fully developed . . .'

As she continues to read we cut to the next scene,
maintaining her voice OOV.

2   Ext. Urban Street. Day. Wedding Shop.   2

A shop-lined street. AMANDA is on her way to school,
heading towards a bus stop. But something catches her eye,
causing her to pause. From her viewpoint we see a bridal
shop.

Stiff-limbed dummies stand in the window, decked out in
white wedding dresses, their hands extended in gestures of
mute supplication.

AMANDA is now in front of the window, face pressed to the
glass.

As the camera pans over the waxen faces of the dummies,
the plastic bouquets and cascades of white frothy lace, we
continue KATHERINE'S VOICE OOV . . .

KATHERINE   (*VO*) 'The brain and spinal chord are still
            growing, as are the jaw and mouth . . .'

The glazed eyes of the bridal dummies stare vacantly out at us.

KATHERINE   (*VO*) 'The head of the foetus is still very large in
            proportion to the rest of the body. The eyes and
            inner ear are developing. The nostrils are
            formed . . .'

And we return, sporadically, to see AMANDA'S FACE pressed against the glass window as the voice over persists.

For a moment we should see her face amongst the wax dummies, in the shop, made up to look just like them, hands clutching a bouquet, veil falling over shoulders, that same vacant smile on her face.

Suddenly she is part of the white, downy world behind the shop window . . . All lace and flowers and sugar and spice.

    KATHERINE (*VO, cont.*) 'The face is just recognisable. The
                    limbs are developing in a rudimentary form . . .

Holding on the wide-eyed, waxen face of AMANDA, transposed by happiness, we cut to:

3   Int. Bedroom. Day. Studio.   3

KATHERINE'S FACE.

Pallid, grey. Dreadily regarding her reflection in the mirror. A stark contrast to the preceding image of her sister.

Hold on her face a moment, before cutting to:

4   Ext. School Playground. Day.   4

The playground, swollen with PUPILS. A riot of activity, particularly at one end of the play area, where a congregation of girls are forming. Led by HILARY, flamboyant in coloured boots and hair to match. Placards are being hoisted into the air. Each one home-made, but boldly inscribed.

Slogans like:

'Equal Education means Equal Classes'

'Girls are more than pretty faces . . . '

'Girls want careers too!'

'We demand the right to choose!'

It is mostly sixth-form girls holding the placards.

Nearby, and unobserved by the girls, a group of fourth- and fifth-year boys are forming. There is something ominous about them, as they jeer and leer at the protesting girls.

We cut now, to see that we have been observing the scene from . . .

5   Int. Classroom. Day.   5

POLLY and AMANDA are hanging out of a window, watching the scene in the playground below.

> AMANDA Now what's happening?

> POLLY They're doing it, they're putting the banner up . . . Prats.

AMANDA glances at her.

> AMANDA Last week you were all for joining them.

> POLLY (*Pointedly*) I meant the boys. Look at them.

AMANDA cranes out to get a better vantage point.

5A   Playground. Day. Ext.   5A

Some of the BOYS have collected a wheelbarrow a gardener has left nearby; they are piling sods of earth into it.

Then they proceed to covertly approach the protesting GIRLS from behind . . .

5B   Int. Locker Room. Day.   5B

> POLLY Creeps. (*She starts to shout, cupping her hands around her mouth*) Watch out . . . behind you . . . !

AMANDA   They'll never hear you.

POLLY   Behind you!!

*But AMANDA is right. The GIRLS are too busy chanting to hear
POLLY's warnings.*

POLLY   I'm going down.

AMANDA   You'll be late for class.

POLLY   Tough! Someone's got to go.

POLLY hurtles off. As she does so, she knocks over a pile of
school textbooks AMANDA has placed on a bench.

AMANDA stoops to pick the books up, when shouts from the
direction of the playground cause her to pause and return to
the window.

5C   Ext. Playground Day.   5C

Below, all hell is breaking loose. The BOYS are lobbing clods
of earth at the GIRLS, who are using their placards as shields.

POLLY is there with them, occasionally picking up a clod of
earth and hurling it back at the BOYS.

As we watch, the placards get torn and battered as the BOYS
continue to pelt them. The various slogans splintering and
tearing under the onslaught.

5D   Int. Locker Room. Day.   5D

A shot of AMANDA'S FACE.

A kind of dawning anger there, as she watches. As if a
distant penny is about to drop.

AMANDA   (*Barely audible, to herself*) She's right, they are
creeps. (*She leans out the window, cupping her
hands like Polly before her*) Creeps! Cowards!

She is about to add to the diatribe, when she suddenly stops.

There is a BOY reflected in the window. His name is GARY.

He is standing behind her. It is the boy we saw in Episode One.

Open-mouthed, AMANDA turns to look at him.

He has some of the books POLLY knocked onto the floor in his hand and he now holds them out to her. A shy romantic smile playing round his mouth.

And the sounds from the playground dissipate into a muted, romantic hum. Suddenly everything is once again in photograph form.

5E   Fantasy Sequence.   5E

We are in another fantasy.

GARY looks at AMANDA one hand extended, holding the books. She looks at him, wide-eyed, that vacant waxen look there again.

GARY  Yours I think.

AMANDA Thank you.

He smiles again.

GARY 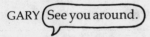 See you around.

He moves away. Hold on AMANDA'S FACE. The photographic effects evaporate.

5F   Int. Locker Room. Day.   5F

We're back in real time.

PATTI'S DISC appears right of frame. Accompanied by a low whistle of appreciation.

> PATTI They're not all creeps are they? You've cracked it there, love. He's made the first move, it's up to you to make the next one. Right?

Shot of AMANDA'S FACE.

6   Int. Locker Room/Factory. Day.   6

Metal lockers line the room. A basin and mirror at one end, a broom cupboard and lavatory at the other. This is the locker room in the factory where Katherine works.

And it is KATHERINE we open on. Now in her factory uniform: she is surrounded by five or six other GIRLS, all similarly attired. Most are aged about eighteen or nineteen, but heavy make-up and the unbecoming uniforms should make them seem older.

KATHERINE's face, like AMANDA's before her, is full of anticipation.

We pull out to see the GIRLS are clustered excitedly around a table, on which are several wrapped presents. The atmosphere is charged and excited. Much nudging and giggling.

Only three of the assembled girls need speak. They are called, SUE, MICHELLE and COREEN respectively.

KATHERINE starts swiftly to unwrap the first present. The GIRLS jostle about her, to get a good look.

> SUE Someone's been splashing out.

> MICHELLE It's not the size, it's the quality, love.

The remark provokes a good deal of sniggering and nudging amongst the GIRLS.

KATHERINE pulls the gift from its wrapping. It's an electric toaster. The GIRLS promptly go into raptures of enthusiasm, mostly manifesting as coos and ahhhhhs.

KATHERINE reads the card accompanying the present and turns to SUSAN . . .

KATHERINE It's lovely, really lovely . . . You shouldn't have . . .

SUSAN You only get married once don't you? You'd better; I'm not coughing up that lot again.

MICHELLE Now mine, come on.

KATHERINE turns back to the presents.

Cut to her eager hands, impatiently clawing at the wrapping paper. The last gift finally emerges, it is a saucy short white nightie. Real Penthouse stuff. Shrieks and sniggers accompany it.

KATHERINE holds it against herself.

KATHERINE Who's bright idea was this?

COREEN All of us . . . not complaining are you?

MICHELLE I'll bet Terry won't at any rate.

This remark, predictably, provokes more nudging and giggling.

The sound of a siren splits into the revelry.

MICHELLE Oy oy. Stand by your beds girls. Time we weren't here.

SUSAN You'd better lock that lot up, love, before someone takes a shine to 'em.

KATHERINE Thank you. All of you.

Swiftly, even tearfully, KATHERINE embraces each girl. It is a genuine moment, not simply of appreciation, but of something else. As if they all sense, inwardly and unconsciously, that this might well be the start of a new chapter for KATHERINE, but it is the end of something as well.

One by one the GIRLS drift back to the factory floor. We hold on KATHERINE looking down at the array of gifts, a confusion of emotions in her face.

MICHELLE lingers a moment by the door. She looks at KATHERINE curiously.

> MICHELLE What is this? Second thoughts: (*Katherine shakes her head*) What then? (*A small shrug from Katherine by way of reply*) It'll be all right on the night, you'll see. (*This at least causes Katherine to grin. Michelle moves to finger the gifts on the table*) I envy you in a way. (*Katherine looks at her quizzically*) Kid on the way . . . a husband . . . home of your own . . . While the rest of us are still knocking about hoping for something better to come along, or *someone* better, you're all set up, aren't you? (*A beat*) Set up for life.

KATHERINE'S FACE, that confusion still evident.

A final shot of the gifts on the table before we cut to:

7   Int. Amanda's Bedroom. Evening. Studio.   7

The room is much as we last saw it.

The photograph of TERRY on the dressing table, the magazines strewn over the bed, KATHERINE's guide to pregnancy on the chair.

But hanging on the outside of the wardrobe is a white satin wedding dress . . . slightly old-fashioned perhaps, but definitely romantic in style.

AMANDA catches sight of the pregnancy book. She picks it up curiously, and examines the drawing of the eight week-old foetus.

Then she sees the wedding dress and all thoughts of the book perish. She puts it down and moves to take the dress from its hanger.

Now she stands in front of the dressing-table mirror, the wedding dress held against her. From her expression we should feel she likes what she sees.

8   Int. Amanda's Sitting Room. Evening.   8
   Studio.

KATHERINE, gathering up the remainder of the wedding gifts.

Like AMANDA before her, her attention is caught by something. The television, which flickers away in one corner. An advertisement for a household cleaner is on.

8A   Int. Commercial. Day. Studio.   8A

We see A GIRL, looking remarkably like KATHERINE, with dishevelled hair, a face free of make-up and adornment, dressed in a wrung-out pinafore, sitting miserably at a kitchen table.

A suitable jingle accompanies the picture. And the usual mid-atlantic drawl of a voice-over.

This is what it is saying:

ADVERT.
VOICE OVER   Is your marriage turning into an Old Wives'
Tale? (*The girl in the picture nods soulfully*) Don't
let dirty dishes TRAP you. Household chores
ENSLAVE you! (*The girl stares hopefully into
camera*) Now CLEAN-UP-TIME gives a new
meaning to women's liberation!

Suddenly the GIRL springs into life. Flinging off her pinafore
to reveal a sexy little dress beneath, shaking free her hair like
a waterfall.

And she dances and cavorts around the kitchen, spraying
everything in sight with an aerosol spray.

ADVERT.
VOICE OVER   (*Cont.*) Yes, only CLEAN-UP-TIME's unique
cleansing action can leave you totally free!

Now a shot of the woman serving supper to her husband (TERRY)

ADVERT.
VOICE OVER   Free to spend time with your husband . . .

*Now a shot of the WOMAN on her hands and knees picking up bits of
food her child has flung to the ground in a tantrum.*

ADVERT.
VOICE OVER   Your children . . .

Now a shot of the WOMAN knee deep in ironing.

ADVERT.
VOICE OVER   Your hobbies . . .   Yes Girls, CLEAN-UP-TIME
is no Old Wives' Tale, it's Women's Liberation
at its best.

*And the frame freezes on the GIRL, swirling around her gleaming
kitchen, her face wearing an unwholesome leer.*

8B   Int. Amanda's Sitting Room. Day.   8B

Abruptly KATHERINE moves to the television and switches it
off. As if she too finds the image of the girl unwholesome . . .
or at best, unaccountably disconcerting.

    MICHAEL   Oy, I was watching that.

Hastily KATHERINE picks up the wedding gifts and exits,
nearly colliding with AMANDA, who is just entering.

AMANDA who stands, staring curiously after her departing
sister, before turning to look around the room, as if it might
hold the answer to some unspoken, but gradually dawning
question.

    MICHAEL   Turn the telly on, Mand.

9   Ext. Amanda's House. Day.   9

Early morning. A milk float perhaps, droning drearily up the
street.

OOV, we can hear KATHERINE'S VOICE, reading aloud from
her pregnancy manual. It is this which leads us gently into
the following scene.

  KATHERINE   (*VO*) 'By the ninth week the foetus is rapidly
               maturing. The eyes and eye lids are now
               developed. Growth of the inner ear and the
               mouth still continues.'

10   Int. Amanda's Bedroom. Day. Studio.   10

AMANDA and KATHERINE, in their respective beds.

KATHERINE, propped up on pillows, reading aloud to her sister. AMANDA lies, drinking tea, listening.

OOV, distantly, the milk float and the sounds of the radio, emanating from the kitchen below.

> KATHERINE 'The nose is quite recognisable. The limbs are also developing rapidly, hands and feet have taken on a rudimentary shape. Sometimes the beginnings of fingers and toes can be discerned.'

11   Ext. School Playground. Day.   11

We see AMANDA and POLLY sitting on a bench. POLLY is watching the Sixth Formers. AMANDA is immersed in a copy of LOVE LIFE.

We see a brief shot of a photo-strip love story. A boy and girl clasped within a heart motif.

We allow KATHERINE'S VOICE to become submerged and lost to us, amongst the noise and bustle of the playground.

We cut now, to see HILARY approaching POLLY and AMANDA.

A girl is with her, whom we shall call JO. An earnest, and over-anxious kind of girl.

They pause, standing over the two younger girls. HILARY reaches out a purple finger-nailed hand and grabs AMANDA's magazine.

> AMANDA   Oy, I happen to be reading that.

> HILARY   Just looking, love.

She flips through the magazine, JO peering over her shoulder. She puts on a mock romantic drawl.

HILARY (*Cont.*) If you want to make me happy Michael,
just hold me. Hold me as if you'll never let
me go.

*A brief shot of AMANDA'S FACE, flushed and angry. AMANDA
then turns, proudly extending a hand out for her magazine.*

AMANDA If you've quite finished.

HILARY We haven't, as it happens. (*She unceremoniously
tosses the magazine back at Amanda as she speaks*)
We're thinking of striking.

AMANDA (*Puzzled*) Striking?

JO (*In her earnest way*) Refusing to attend classes.
The school won't discuss our demands, won't
even agree to meet to talk about them, so we're
thinking of striking until they do.

HILARY And we want you to back us.

*AMANDA and POLLY look at one another. A slight pause. JO looks
from one to the other.*

JO Well?

AMANDA (*Sullenly, the kind born of pride*) I'll think about it.

HILARY In other words you'd rather sit on the fence?

AMANDA If that's what you want to call it.

HILARY (*To POLLY*) Does she do the talking for you too,
or what?

*AMANDA looks at POLLY, who glances at her a moment, and then
rises.*

POLLY No. (*Then*) You can count me in.

HILARY walks off with POLLY.

Once again, AMANDA'S FACE, watching her departing
friend.

JO, however, makes no attempt to follow them, rather she lingers over AMANDA, as if sensing something of her dilemma and pride.

JO   It's all in a good cause you know.

AMANDA   Oh sure. (*Her voice is taut and slightly insolent*) And I'm sure it makes you all feel very important as well. *I* just don't happen to think it is.

JO   You think we're enjoying it, do you? Walking around with those things? Placards? Everyone laughing at us? Missing classes, threatening our exams, everything! (*Amanda says nothing*) It's not just important in itself, there's an important principle involved. If you can't see that you're as . . . (*Her eye catches sight of the magazine*) . . . blinkered and stupid as those pathetic girls you enjoy reading about so much.

JO swings around on her heel and walks off.

AMANDA looks at her a moment, and then down, at the magazine in her hands.

As she does, PATTI'S DISC appears to the right hand of screen, attempting to attract the somewhat distracted AMANDA.

PATTI   Amanda? Oh Amanda? (*Then*) Forget her. It's your life, remember? Come on.

AMANDA glances around, to see the BOY featured earlier, standing a little distance away.

He is simply standing, shyly yet casually, looking in AMANDA's direction.

PATTI   Come on, give him a smile.

AMANDA, hesitantly, allows a small smile to play around her lips.

While AMANDA busies herself thus, we once more allow a romantic haze to envelope the picture.

The noise and swirl of the playground are replaced by the photographic effects. . .

11A Fantasy. Playground.   11A

It should seem, to us as well as to AMANDA, that no one else exists at that moment, except for GARY and herself, smiling coyly at each other over the expanse of playground which separates them.

AMANDA: She's right. He really is special. I wonder what he's thinking . . .

We see GARY gazing at her. We are in cartoon form.

GARY: Boy! She's quite something. This might just be my lucky day!

We are jerked back from the fantasy into live action.

11B Ext. School Playground.   11B

AMANDA turns to see the placard-waving girls, led by JO. They are mutely playing violins, miming grotesquely at her, in gestures clearly intended to extract the Michael.

And so the romance of the moment is shattered.

AMANDA turns, angry but also not a little hurt, to march away. And as the GIRLS cat call and yell after her, we hold on POLLY, watching her departure. A look of guilt about her.

12   Int. Locker Room. Day.   **12**

It's the end of the day, as we can tell by the hoards of GIRLS hurtling to fling open lockers.

We pick out AMANDA amongst them, at her own locker. Pictures of pop stars are taped inside the door.

AMANDA is sorting through some books and collecting her outdoor coat. As she does so, we catch sight of POLLY behind her: hesitating, as if uncertain as to her reception. POLLY decides to brazen it out.

> POLLY   What bus are you getting?

> AMANDA   Usual.

> POLLY   You fancy coming to my place for a while? Killing a few hours?

AMANDA says nothing for a moment.

> AMANDA   I thought you'd be on the picket line or something.

> POLLY   Come on, Mandy.

> AMANDA   'Come on Mandy' what? They're your big buddies now aren't they? (*More abruptly perhaps, than she intends*) Anyway, I can't. I'm meeting Katherine. She's going to show me her new flat.

And we hold on POLLY, looking ruefully after her.

13   Ext. School Gate.   **13**

The clump of Sixth Formers, at their position at the school gates, placards in hands.

We see AMANDA striding purposefully by them, steadfastly keeping eyes to the ground.

A swift shot of HILARY, watching her go by.

And now we see POLLY, running to catch up with AMANDA. Pausing only momentarily by the congregation of girls and banners, before looking at her departing friend, and following her.

For a moment both girls walk along side by side in silence. It is left to POLLY to take the initiative.

> POLLY   How is she anyway? (*As Amanda glances at her*) Katherine . . . ?

> AMANDA   OK.

> POLLY   She's got guts, I'll say that for her.

> AMANDA   (*Puzzled*) Guts?

> POLLY   Going through with it all. (*As Amanda continues to look puzzled*) The baby and everything. She needn't, need she? No one has to, not these days.

AMANDA stops in her tracks to stare at her.

> AMANDA   How can you even think such a thing?

> POLLY   Why not? It's not like it's an individual or anything, is it? Not this early.

> AMANDA   It's still a baby!

> POLLY   Do me a favour.

> AMANDA   Of course it is! Anyway, she happens to want it.

> POLLY   Or she thinks she does.

AMANDA regards her icily for a moment, before striding angrily off. Leaving POLLY once again watching her, but this time, making no attempt to follow her.

14   Ext. Council Tower Block. Day.   14

We are looking up at a grey, monolithic slab of a tower block.
Already stained by the elements and the inevitable graffiti. It
looks both unyielding and unwelcoming. We cut, to see
KATHERINE and AMANDA looking up at it. And then around
them, at the bleak urban landscape, the KIDS playing
amongst the parked cars. A careworn WOMAN, pushing a
pram, passes by.

Both girls watch her, before wanly looking up at the concrete
slab above them.

> KATHERINE   (*Determined to be cheerful*) Well it's the inside that
> counts isn't it?

AMANDA smiles but says nothing.

15   Int. Katherine's Flat. Day. Studio.   15

AMANDA is standing on a chair, measuring the window for
curtains.

We get a chance to see the interior of the flat now. It does
look more than a little bleak, but then it is, as yet, bereft of
furnishing and fittings.

For a moment AMANDA and KATHERINE work in silence.
AMANDA glances around the room.

> KATHERINE   (*Quickly*) A bit of paint and wallpaper, it'll be
> really smashing . . . And it's a smashing view.

> AMANDA   Oh on a clear day you can even see the airport.

KATHERINE, in spite of herself, laughs.

> AMANDA   No, it's great, of course it is. You're dead lucky
> to get it.

KATHERINE   Luck didn't come into it. Terry's uncle pulled a few strings with the Housing Department. Said he wanted us to have the best possible start in life.

But there is something about the way KATHERINE says it, which denies the words.

16   Int. Amanda's Sitting Room. Evening.   16
Studio.

KATHERINE is standing on the coffee table.

She is wearing the white wedding dress we saw hanging in her room. Her MOTHER is kneeling, cutting down the hem.

JUNE   Try and hold still, Katherine, this isn't easy you know.

KATHERINE   Sorry.

We cut, to see AMANDA watching from the depths of an armchair.

AMANDA   Did you really wear it for your wedding Mum?

JUNE   I most certainly did. And I saved it for just this occasion. (*She nods towards the mantlepiece*) See for yourself.

AMANDA rises to look at the photograph. We should see it from her viewpoint. Her MOTHER and FATHER, looking no older than KATHERINE and TERRY, arm in arm, outside a church.

AMANDA   It seems awful, cutting it down.

JUNE   It's more suitable for a registry office wedding, isn't it? She doesn't want to be overdressed.

AMANDA   Why does it have to be a registry office wedding anyway? Why can't it be in a church with a proper ceremony and things?

KATHERINE Because for one thing I haven't set foot in a church since the day you were christened. And for another, a white wedding with all the trimmings in my condition would be just a mite hypocritical, wouldn't you say? (*Her mother glances sharply at her*) Look, even with her crummy maths she'll be able to work it out for herself after it's born, won't she? Everyone will.

Abruptly JUNE rises and exits.

KATHERINE, angrily but a touch remorsefully, scrambles down off the table.

  KATHERINE Mother?

She exits after JUNE.

We hold on AMANDA, who turns to look at the wedding photograph. Her MOTHER, poignantly youthful in the wedding dress, smiling with shy optimism at the camera.

17   Int. Sitting Room. Night. Studio.   17

The wedding photograph again. This time, lit differently, from table lamps and perhaps the flicker of a coal fire in the grate.

JUNE is sewing the wedding dress. As she sews, she talks, now and again glancing at the wedding photograph.

  JUNE And it rained, do you remember? Well, showered . . . And your mother started on about it being bad luck and goodness knows what. (*Pause*) And she found that hip flask in your father's back pocket and they rowed all through the reception. (*A silence, her needle darting in and out of the hem, the crackle from the fire*) And I cried in the toilet like a school girl because I knew a part of my life was over and I wasn't sure what lay ahead. Silly isn't it, letting the most important day in a girl's life be ruined by a few childish fears.

She glances up, and we cut, to see FRANK.

He is asleep in his armchair. Head thrown back, mouth agape, oblivious to his wife and the world in general.

JUNE looks at him a moment before returning to her sewing.

18   Int. Amanda's Bedroom. Night. Studio.   18

KATHERINE, lying in the darkened bedroom, clearly unable to sleep.

We hold on her, restlessly tossing, before eventually relinquishing all hopes for sleep and simply lying motionless. There is something almost apprehensive about her expression.

19   Ext. Amanda's House.   19

Two cars, with white streamers on the bonnets are parked outside the house.

AMANDA, her brother MICHAEL and PARENTS can be seen hovering and waiting at the garden gate. A few curious onlookers and well-wishers are also present.

Eventually KATHERINE emerges, the white wedding dress now knee-length.

Her PARENTS coo and cluck around her, and as they hurry to the waiting cars we cut to:

20   Int. Wedding Car. Day. Film.   20

AMANDA, also smartly dressed, is sitting next to MICHAEL and JUNE.

As the car pauses at some lights, she glances out of the window. They happen to be outside the bridal shop, featured earlier. Those waxen brides beaming wide-eyed out at us.

AMANDA'S FACE, watching them.

And now, a star-light filter kind of effect. The picture shimmers and the sound ebbs. To be replaced by another sound. That of a VICAR, voicing a wedding ceremony.

> VICAR'S
> VOICE OVER Dearly beloved, we are gathered here in the sight of God, and in the face of this congregation . . .

Mix to:

21   Fantasy. Int. Church. Day. Film.   21

A shimmering, romantic haze envelopes everything.

A BRIDE, her face obscured from us, stands next to the GROOM in front of the VICAR. BRIDE and GROOM have their backs to us. Soft organ music tinkles in the background.

Through the glistening, glimmering translucent light we can dimly discern the outlines of the wedding congregation.

The camera seems to dive and float as it moves towards the VICAR, and BRIDE and GROOM. The VICAR's VOICE OVER, gently echoing around the splendid and gothic interior of the church.

> VICAR (*VO*) . . . to join together this Man and this Woman in holy Matrimony, which is an honourable estate, instituted of God himself signifying unto us the mystical union . . .

A very different atmosphere. We are in the spartan and clinical atmosphere of the registry office.

KATHERINE and TERRY sit rather nervously in front of a large square table.

A squat, middle-aged spectacled man, the REGISTRAR, is conducting the service. He has a brisk, business-like manner, reminiscent of a bank manager.

AMANDA'S FAMILY, including herself, sit rather awkwardly to one side of the table.

TERRY'S FAMILY sit at the other side.

We pick up the Registrar mid-way through the ceremony . . .

REGISTRAR . . . according to the law of this country is the union of one man and one woman, voluntarily entered into for life to the exclusion of all others . . .

AMANDA'S FACE, watching. A far-away look on her face.

Cut to:

23   Fantasy. Int. Church. Day. Film.   23

The romantic haze of the church wedding again.

We are looking straight at the BRIDE, but her face is barely visible under the cascade of lace and veil obscuring it.

VICAR . . . To live together according to God's law in the holy estate of Matrimony?

Cut to:

24   Int. Registry Office. Day. Studio.   24

REGISTRAR   I do solemnly declare . . .

TERRY   I do solemnly declare . . .

REGISTRAR   That I know not of any impediment . . .

TERRY   That I know not of any impediment . . .

Cut to:

25   Fantasy. Int. Church. Day. Film.   25

VICAR   Wilt thou love her, comfort her, honour and
keep her in sickness and in health?

Cut to:

26   Int. Registry Office. Day. Studio.   26

REGISTRAR   I call upon these persons here present . . .

TERRY   I call upon these persons here present . . .

REGISTRAR   To witness . . .

Cut to:

27   Fantasy. Int. Church. Day. Film.   27

VICAR   (*To Bride*) Wilt thou obey him, and serve him.
love, honour and keep him in sickness and in
health?

Cut to:

28   Int. Registry Office. Day. Studio.   28

REGISTRAR You are now joined as husband and wife . . .

Cut to:

29   Fantasy. Int. Church. Day. Film.   29

VICAR . . . I pronounce that they be Man and Wife together. In the name of the Father and of the Son and the Holy Ghost. Amen.

As the organ music swells to a crescendo, The BRIDE turns to the GROOM.

The veil is lifted. AMANDA'S FACE is revealed.

Cartoon effects and a bubble appears above AMANDA'S HEAD.

AMANDA  Oh, if this day could last forever . . . !

And now the GROOM slowly turns to her. It is GARY, the boy from school.

As he bends forward to kiss her, and she tilts her head to receive his kiss, cut to:

30   Int. Registry Office. Day. Studio.   30

We are back in real time.
TERRY, briefly kissing KATHERINE. The REGISTRAR, closing the book. the GUESTS shifting awkwardly. We cut to JUNE, standing near FRANK and AMANDA.

REGISTRAR Congratulations.

JUNE It's quickly done, I'll say that.

She says it with an air of disappointment.

FRANK Not so quickly undone though.

As JUNE and AMANDA turn to look at him, cut to:

31 Int. Sitting Room. Day. Studio. 31

TERRY, his tie askew and hair dishevelled, is brandishing a glass of scotch.

MICHAEL, FRANK and other male GUESTS surround him. All are the worse for alcohol. But you'd never know it from the lustiness of their voices as they noisily chorus some football song together.

We cut to see AMANDA, in the doorway. She watches a moment, before withdrawing to the hall.

32 Int. Hall. Day. Studio. 32

AMANDA, clearly at a loose end, and not a little bored, prods open the kitchen door.

Within we can see JUNE and one or two female guests and relatives.

JUNE is packing up the wedding dress into a box. She looks tearful, and sounds it.

> JUNE It's just weddings . . . they always bring out the sentiment in me. (*She closes the lid of the box*) I suppose the next time I'll get this out will be for Amanda.

Hold on AMANDA'S FACE.

Cut to:

33 Int. Amanda's Bedroom. Day. Studio. 33

KATHERINE, in a smart suit, is packing up a case. She picks

up the pregnancy guide and glances at it a moment, before putting into the case and snapping it shut.

AMANDA enters. They glance at each other a moment.

> KATHERINE Well, this is it. Scarborough here we come.
> (*She glances around the room*) I never thought I'd be sorry to see the last of this room . . .
> (*Amanda's face*) You'll have to go it on your own from now on. No more big sister to cramp your style.

But her words are denied by the obvious emotion behind them.

Suddenly AMANDA moves, to put her arms around KATHERINE.

> KATHERINE I'd better go. We'll miss that train.

She disengages from AMANDA and picks up her case.

> AMANDA Kath?

KATHERINE, now at the door, pauses.

> AMANDA You are happy aren't you? (*There is a sudden urgency about the way she says it*)

> KATHERINE (*After a moment*) What do you think?

And on that ambiguous note, she goes.

34   Ext. Amanda's House. Day.   34

KATHERINE and TERRY, cases in hand, emerge from the house, quickly followed by FRIENDS and FAMILY, who shower them with confetti.

As they run to one of the waiting wedding cars, we pan upwards. We see AMANDA'S FACE, framed in her bedroom window. We hold on her face. Unlike that of her family, it is not smiling. Rather it should be reminiscent of KATHERINE's, the eve of the wedding. An unmistakable look of apprehension about it.

On that, we freeze frame, and bring up PATTI'S FACE, beaming and leering, right of screen.

PATTI Is Amanda beginning to see the light?

Can Katherine weather the storms ahead?

And will Gary ever pop the question?

To be continued . . . next week.

End of Episode Two

A closer look at . . .

The family

When you are a child the people you live with, those who care for you, are the most important people in your life. When you are growing up you are very much influenced by what they say and do. Arguments and conflicts do occur, but they tend to be minor ones and easily solved. Children often confide in their parents, telling them about their day, their friends, and their feelings. Why does this situation seem to change when you reach adolescence? Why do parent–child relationships become more complex, and apparently fraught with difficulties?

Do your parents really know you? If they were to describe you, how accurate would you find their description? Many of you will have thoughts and feelings which you keep secret from your parents – a whole private world inside your head. This may be because you think they will not understand, or they may judge you. Have you ever had this conversation with one of your family?

> A Hello, love. Had a good day at school?
> B Alright.
> A What did you do?
> B Nothing much.
> A Going out tonight?
> B Don't know. Might do.
> A Where are you going?
> B Nowhere special.

Most people have fobbed their family off with 'non-answers' like this at some time. Does it sound familiar? How does your family react if you do not talk to them as you once did? You may feel more distant from your parents and they probably feel more distant from you.

Going through one's teens can be a difficult time. Teenagers change and develop very quickly, both physically and emotionally. They are no longer children to be guided almost totally by the adults around them. Nor are they adults, able to make completely independent decisions. What kind of restrictions are placed on you? Why are they there? Do you feel you need and deserve more freedom than you have?

Try to put yourself in your parents' position: what are you like to live with? What kind of problems and worries do you cause them? It is very easy to think of parents as 'just parents', only existing in the way you perceive them, and always having been that way. But the people you live with are not just 'Mum' or 'Dad'. Think of all the forms of address applied to the person you know as 'Mum' (Sheila, Mrs Black, Madam, darling, love, Auntie, and so on). What do these signify? Parents have a personality and a life of their own. They too will have a secret world inside their heads, full of hopes, dreams, insecurities and fears. Your parents were living, thinking, and having good times and bad times long before you were born.

There comes a time in everyone's life when they begin to see parents as real people with virtues and faults rather than just Mum and Dad. When did this happen to you? What do you hope your relationship with your family will be like in the future, say in ten years' time? What could you do to help make it that way?

EPISODE THREE

'And Baby makes Three'

Synopsis

Katherine is about to have her baby, but her doubts persist. At school a sixth-form feminist is activating a campaign for equality in the classroom. Although tempted to join them, Amanda is being increasingly pressured by Patti, to aspire to the rosy romance depicted in her teenage magazines.

In the meantime, her brother Michael arranges a date with her best friend, Polly. At thirteen feelings run high and it seems friendship can fade overnight. Amanda resolves to follow Patti's beckoning finger towards a relationship of her own.

1   Int. Ante-Natal Clinic. Day. Studio.   1

A rumble of activity. Voices. Distantly a telephone ringing . . . the sound of typing . . . lift doors clanging.

We close in on a pile of magazines, piled haphazardly on a table. The image of them should fill the screen. Some, largely obscured at the bottom, are the *Woman's Weekly* and *Woman's Own* variety. But mostly visible are our teenage romantic love-strip magazines.

1A   Standard Int. Magazine Montage.   1A

The by-now familiar images of distraught girls and lanky long-haired lads in skin-tight jeans and medallions . . . kissing, cuddling, caressing . . .

Now the sounds build, as in previous episodes, and the camera roves over the balloons and bubbles.

Voices, husky with emotion, obliterate the other sounds . . .

And the voices, as before, bleed into one another, in a distorted crescendo.

Amongst the balloons and baby-faced girls, bring up the titles:

1B   Sub-title   1B

Bring up the episode title:

Episode Three, And Baby makes Three.

Abruptly the ragged chorus of voices recede, as another supersedes them . . .

1C   Ante-Natal Clinic. Day. Studio.   1C

NURSE Gayfer, Wynbourne, Tryant, Hughes . . .

We cut to see a NURSE, dressed in the uniform of a Sister, at one end of the ante-natal clinic. She has a clipboard of notes in one hand. An ageless, tireless efficiency about her.

She barks the names out unceremoniously. It's clearly a procedure she's been through many times before.

Now we cut to see the clinic itself. We're in a large waiting area, lined with chairs and benches.

The atmosphere is the usual one of institutional anonymity. Grey painted walls are covered in posters, proclaiming the value of vitamin pills for pregnant women, and the evils of smoking.

The room is thronging (at least that should be the impression) with PREGNANT WOMEN. Ponderous abdomens to the fore, sitting waiting, with attitudes of calculated forebearance.

A group of these WOMEN now rise, to waddle towards the NURSE. They go behind a curtained area at the end, and are lost to us.

We cut now, to see AMANDA. A love-strip magazine inevitably on lap, seated amidst the rows of PREGNANT WOMEN.

She looks to the right of her, to see an army of rounded, football-like stomachs, stretching, it should seem, as far as the eye can see.

And now she looks to the left of her where KATHERINE sits . . . and beyond, another row of swollen stomachs . . .

AMANDA'S GLANCE moves on, to a poster on the wall . . . A pregnant girl, hazily and romantically shot, stands attractively by a window, her liberty print smock clinging becomingly, one hand, proprietorially on her stomach. Underneath it explains the value of regular ante-natal care, *A Safe Pregnancy is a Happy One*, or whatever.

AMANDA catches KATHERINE's eye and smiles.

We should observe that KATHERINE is well advanced in her pregnancy. She is enormous, and looks and clearly feels, fatigued and acutely uncomfortable. None of that 'bloom of pregnancy' rot about *her*.

KATHERINE looks around at the pregnant women surrounding her.

  KATHERINE Like a ruddy cattle market.

AMANDA too turns to look at the women. As she does so, KATHERINE's hand moves involuntarily to her abdomen.

   AMANDA Alright?

  KATHERINE Fine. Never better.

And all the time we should be aware of the hospital humming about them. White coats shifting in the distance. Nurses padding in and out of doors.

The clinic SISTER reappears, clipboard at the ready.

> NURSE   Georgeson, Maynard, Tailor, Saunders . . .

More women cumbersomely rise to waddle off. KATHERINE is amongst them.

> KATHERINE   (*As she goes*) About time.

KATHERINE lumbers off. AMANDA watches. We hold on her face, as the voices of two nearby PREGNANT WOMEN attract her attention.

One, in her late thirties, has a dishevelled, unkempt look about her. She is surrounded by shopping bags, toys and a double pushchair. The children, we can assume, are off exploring somewhere.

The other one is younger, less pregnant, a look of optimism still evident in her expression.

They clearly haven't met before, but their common condition and the interminable wait breaks all social barriers on these occasions.

> OLDER
> WOMAN   I didn't plan it this way. With three already and the youngest not out of nappies only a lunatic would go into it again, wouldn't they? (*The second girl smiles politely*) My fault, I should have been more careful, I was still breast feeding and I thought that would stop it . . . some hope.

> SECOND
> GIRL   Well, it'll round the family off nicely anyway.

> OLDER
> WOMAN   And the bills. Cost a fortune, you know, kids. Food, clothes, toys . . . and the shoes! The price of them! You have to slog all day at some rotten job to keep them all, and then you never get to see 'em. Where's the sense in that?

AMANDA'S FACE, intently listening.

OLDER
WOMAN   (*Glancing at the younger girl*) Your first is it?

SECOND
GIRL   Yes. (*Pause*) We're terribly excited . . .

OLDER
WOMAN   Oh it is exciting, first time round. No doubt
about it. After that it's a different story.

The other GIRL smiles in polite amusement.

We return to AMANDA'S FACE. She looks away, up at the
poster of the romantically pregnant girl, smiling by the open
window. Clearly a dream come true. But a far cry from the
conversation she's just overheard.

---

2   Int. Amanda's Kitchen. Day. Studio.   2

Early evening.

AMANDA is doing homework at the table . . . maths
perhaps, a lot of smudges and crossing out evident. JUNE is
washing up at the sink. Distantly we can hear the sound of
the television from the sitting room.

AMANDA   She doesn't seem very excited about it. (*As her
mother looks at her*) Katherine. She seems so . . .
down.

JUNE doesn't reply immediately. If she has an answer to the
question, she doesn't quite know how to articulate it to her
young daughter. She opts for a common-sense answer
instead.

JUNE   She's just tired. You get that way at the end.

AMANDA   Dad doesn't either. He never talks about it at all
if he can help it.

JUNE   He's not used to the idea yet, that's all.

AMANDA   After all this time.

JUNE hesitates, wiping her hands on a dishcloth.

JUNE   He is excited about the baby, Amanda . . . in his own way. He's just . . . disappointed as well.

AMANDA   (*A perplexed frown there*) Disappointed?

JUNE   That it happened the way it did.

AMANDA   Why does it matter how it happened? So long as it's what Katherine wants?

JUNE   (*Slightly harsher than she intends*) And what about what your father might want? (*She modifies her manner slightly, seeing Amanda look startled*) He had high hopes for Katherine . . . we both did. What do you suppose all those sacrifices were about? All those extra classes? They were an investment in her future, so she could get a decent job . . . travel . . . instead of which she chucks in school at sixteen and gets married by nineteen.

AMANDA says nothing. Reacting perhaps, to the depth of feeling still present in her mother's tone.

JUNE glances at her once again.

JUNE   Still, we're not beaten yet. We'll just have to pin our hopes on you instead, won't we?

AMANDA'S FACE, uncertain at this. The door bell rings, OOV, curtailing the conversation . . .

3   Int. Amanda's Hall. Day. Studio.   3

MICHAEL, swinging downstairs, to answer the door. Seeing a female silhouette through the glass, he pauses, to quickly run a comb through his hair, check his appearance in the mirror.

He seems pleased by what he sees.

He throws open the door, to reveal POLLY. She is in her school uniform. A shoulder bag of books over one arm.

MICHAEL's confidence ebbs slightly. He becomes suddenly shy, bashful even.

>   MICHAEL Hi.

>   POLLY Hi.

A pause, of the awkward kind. As if suddenly, inexplicably, new ground is opening up between them and they are not certain how to handle it.

>   POLLY Er . . . is Mandy about?

>   MICHAEL Sure.

POLLY enters. She starts to lower the school bag to the floor, when MICHAEL promptly steps up.

>   MICHAEL I'll take that.

>   POLLY (*Surprised, but pleasantly so*) Ta.

He hangs the bag on the bannisters and they smile at each other. It's all very coy and embarrassed, as if they are both taken by surprise by this new turn of events.

>   MICHAEL Right . . . in here . . .

And POLLY follows MICHAEL to the kitchen.

4   Int. Amanda's Kitchen. Day. Studio.   4

AMANDA, still stooped over her school books.
JUNE busy in the kitchen area.

>   MICHAEL (*As he enters*) Visitor for you, face-ache.

And it's interesting that his sister merits derision, while her friend commands respect and attention.

AMANDA looks up. A slightly strained atmosphere is obvious between herself and POLLY.

> POLLY Hiya.

> AMANDA Hello.

Clearly their former breach has not entirely healed.

> JUNE Polly . . . how nice. How are you?

> POLLY Oh fine, you know.

> JUNE And your mother?

> POLLY She's fine too.

> JUNE Good. Right, I'm finished. The kettle's on if you want some coffee . . .

> POLLY Thanks.

JUNE goes. MICHAEL, instead of following her, moves to sit down. Lounging in a chair, eyes on POLLY. POLLY goes to the kettle and starts on the coffee.

AMANDA looks at her brother looking at her friend and looks back down – slightly confused.

> POLLY You want some coffee, Michael?

> MICHAEL Why not?

> POLLY Mandy?

> AMANDA (*Tonelessly*) If you're making it. (*She steals another look at her brother, who is still watching Polly. To Polly*) I thought you'd be at one of your demos (*To Michael*) She's all involved with the sixth-year girls, equal rights and all that.

And AMANDA'S TONE clearly suggests that POLLY might
well be regarded as certifiable for such activities, and that her
brother will be quick to agree with her.

> MICHAEL   Yeah? I heard about that. How's it going?

> POLLY   We're still on tactics you know . . . Trying to
> get the teachers on our side.

*During this exchange AMANDA looks at her BROTHER in
astonishment.*

> MICHAEL   Some hope.

> POLLY   We'll get nowhere without them.

*MICHAEL and POLLY smile at one another again, as two people do,
who find they share a cause. AMANDA looks at them both askance.*

> AMANDA   (*To Michael*) Since when have you been so
> interested?

> MICHAEL   Since we had the same aggro at our school.
> Except it was about options, and who decides
> them. The teachers reckon it's finally their
> choice, and we reckon it's ours.

> AMANDA   Hardly the same.

> POLLY   It's exactly the same. They want to be treated as
> individuals and so do we.

*We should sense it's stubbornness and hurt pride which is
preventing AMANDA from acknowledging their argument.*

> AMANDA   (*Returning to her school work*) All this equal rights
> . . . there's too much banner-waving and talk
> if you ask me. Months it's been going on.

> POLLY   That's why I'm here as it happens. (*As Amanda
> glances at her*) We're having a meeting to
> decide on where we go next. Before school,
> tomorrow. Sixth-year common room. OK?

> AMANDA   I've my paper round to do.

MICHAEL You're through that by eight.

POLLY looks pointedly at AMANDA, who lowers her eyes.

AMANDA Alright. If I can.

POLLY Good.

POLLY puts the coffees on the table and sits down.

Once again, both we, and AMANDA, are aware of the electric attraction between POLLY and MICHAEL.

A pause.

POLLY You er . . . been to that new disco at St Alban's Youth Club yet?

MICHAEL No.

POLLY It's great. Great atmosphere. You should come along sometime.

MICHAEL Alright. When?

The directness of the question takes AMANDA aback.

POLLY There's one Thursday night . . .

MICHAEL Right . . . terrific . . . I'll meet you outside . . . say around seven?

POLLY Right.

*Another smile is exchanged, less coy, more one of anticipation.
POLLY turns to AMANDA, who is staring at them both.*

POLLY How about it, Mandy? You coming too?

A pause.

AMANDA (*Slightly tart*) So long as I'm not in anyone's way . . .

MICHAEL smiles amiably at POLLY.

    MICHAEL No chance.

And on POLLY's answering smile, and AMANDA's expression, cut to:

5   Int. Amanda's Bedroom. Night. Studio.   5

AMANDA, lying in bed, the room illuminated by the street lamp.

Above Amanda's bed, and shot from her viewpoint, is a pinboard. Amongst the pop stars and postcards pinned on it, are several snapshots. They depict Polly and Amanda, laughing and giggling together . . . clinging onto a seesaw, grinning into camera . . . riding a tandem bike . . . and those passport type pictures, in strips, the two girls, heads pressed together, leering and beaming at us, arms around each other's shoulders . . .

We return to AMANDA'S FACE, looking at the photographs. Something wistful in her expression.

6   Int. Sixth-Year Common Room. Day. Studio. 6

We see POLLY'S FACE, and AMANDA, sitting a little distance away.

They are surrounded by a group of girls, sitting cross-legged on the floor, on chairs. JO and HILARY are at the front, addressing them.

      HILARY OK, let's recap. And if you don't want to listen – push off – OK? First off we've had a meeting with the teachers, via the school council . . .

          JO (*Intercepting, in her earnest way*) an *informal* meeting . . .

HILARY   Right. An informal meeting. The teachers are sympathetic, but raised a load of practical stuff. Like there not being enough text books or equipment for girls to do technical drawing and woodwork etc. along with the boys. So if we want their support . . .

JO   . . . Formal support . . .

HILARY   (*Slightly weary*) Formal support . . . we've got to get the practical problems out of the way first.

A rumble of dismay from the girls listening.

POLLY   How do we do that?

HILARY   By earning the money to buy them.

As the girls start to jeer at this:

HILARY   Just hear us out. Jo's old man is on the local council. It seems they want a mural painted on that brick wall by the car park, something cheerful to give a good impression of the town . . .

JO   . . . And to discourage the graffiti artists . . .

Catcalls at this.

HILARY   And she's talked her father into putting us up to do it. The council have agreed, providing we can come up with an idea, a plan, they approve of. They'll buy the materials and give us a hundred pounds.

POLLY   Is that all?

HILARY   Have you got any better ideas? We've talked long enough, now it's time to show we mean business.

JO   And it'll be good publicity for us. The local
       press are bound to get hold of it and everyone'll
       know why we did it, won't they?

HILARY   So we need anyone good at art to volunteer.

JO   And those that aren't can help. OK? So roll up
       and give us your names.

No-one moves for a moment.

HILARY   Or perhaps you'd as soon forget the whole
          damn thing?

It's said as a challenge and it works. The GIRLS raggedly start
to rise, POLLY and AMANDA amongst them.

As she does so, AMANDA glances at the door. Framed in the
glass window we see GARY'S FACE, looking curiously at the
assembled girls.

POLLY pauses, *en route* to the queue of GIRLS forming in front
of JO and HILARY.

POLLY   Mandy? Come on! (*Her glance follows Amanda's,
          to Gary's, in the door-window*) Oh for Pete's
          sake . . !

AMANDA tugs her eyes away from GARY, and moves
towards POLLY. They join the tag end of the queue of GIRLS.

But AMANDA's GAZE returns to the doorway. GARY has now
departed.

We hold on her expression, that wistful look there again.

7 Int. Disco. Night. Studio.   7

Crashing, thudding disco music. A swirl of activity on the
floor, as people dancing weave and thread their way around.

Amongst the darting dancers and flashing lights, we pick out POLLY and MICHAEL, dancing together, arms around each others waists, gliding through the teenagers surrounding them . . .

Now we cut, to see AMANDA, nervously at the edge. She looks and feels intimidated, as she watches her brother and friend cavort and wheel about.

We see them from her viewpoint. A romantic haze envelopes them . . .

7A Fantasy. Disco. 7A

We are now into the photographic effects. It is no longer POLLY and MICHAEL dancing . . . it's GARY and AMANDA . . .

Arm-in-arm, eyes on each other's faces. Speech bubbles appear above their heads.

GARY (I'm really glad you could make it, Amanda . . .)

AMANDA (Me too, Gary!)

Now another shot of them, dancing in perfect harmony.

GARY (Hey – you're really good!)

AMANDA (You're not so bad yourself!)

Another shot of them, AMANDA looking mistily into his eyes.

GARY (Make quite a team, don't we?)

AMANDA (I always knew we would!)

Over the diso music and images of them dancing another sound emerges . . . It is POLLY, calling . . .

POLLY Amanda! Hey, Mandy . . !

*AMANDA blinks her eyes . . . Photographic effects disappear
leaving us back in real time.*

7B   Int. Disco. Night. Studio.   7B

POLLY and MICHAEL are swooping down on her.

MICHAEL   You going to stand there all night, or what?

POLLY Come on . . .!

MICHAEL and POLLY hold their hands encouragingly, and
hesitantly. AMANDA goes towards them, tottering on her
high heels.

But someone bumps into her and she reels headlong onto the
ground.

As they burst out laughing, AMANDA rises, flustered and
confused.

8   Int. Katherine's Living Room. Day. Studio.   8

We're in the sitting room of the flat. It's now decorated, and
sparsely furnished.

For all that, it still has a bleak, unwelcoming feel about it, as if
the greyness of the exterior has somehow pervaded the
interior as well.

'KATHERINE is seated on the sofa, crocheting a baby's shawl.
We can hear TERRY rattling about in the kitchen beyond.

The room itself, is in mild disarray. No sign of the
houseproud young bride evident here.

TERRY   (*OOV*) Kath! Where's the lager?

She doesn't reply, and he enters. He is dressed in dirty
overalls. He's a mechanic in a garage.

TERRY   Lager . . . didn't you get any?

KATHERINE   No.

TERRY   Thanks, terrific.

TERRY is about to exit when KATHERINE speaks:

KATHERINE   The lift isn't working. It's half a mile to the nearest shops. What do you expect, Terry? If you wanted it, you should get it in your dinner hour.

TERRY   Dinner hour? What dinner hour? Last week you were on about us having no money so I'm working straight through, aren't I? I've had one hell of a day and I come home to an empty fridge and you in one of your sulks.

KATHERINE   I am not sulking. I'm just not up to running errands for you.

TERRY   Yeah, well I've got a few problems too you know. Like hanging onto my job and earning enough bread to keep us. But you're too wrapped up in yourself to think of that, aren't you?!

He pauses, slightly embarrassed. AMANDA has entered.

AMANDA   The er . . . door was open . . .

TERRY   Well don't expect the red carpet routine. There's no food, no drink and your sister's got a mood on. (*He picks up some car keys*) I'll get us a take-away.

KATHERINE   Don't bother on my account.

TERRY   You've got to eat something for Chrissake!

KATHERINE   I'm not hungry.

TERRY   Alright, go without! Do what you like!

TERRY crashes out. AMANDA looks at the door, to her sister, embarrassed and bewildered.

KATHERINE   It's just the waiting. It's getting to us. We're just not coping with it, so we take it out on each other. Help me up will you?

She puts out a hand, and AMANDA moves, to haul her up. KATHERINE walks, to stand at the window.

AMANDA   Not coping with what?

KATHERINE   Any of it. Responsibility. Parenthood. The whole bit. I look out here, in the mornings sometimes . . . I see girls of my age, younger even, on their way to work . . . meeting people . . . going places. (*Pause*) Then there's all Terry's friends . . . they're all still single. Planning holidays, trips to football matches. He's either stuck at work doing overtime or stuck in here with me going on at him.

AMANDA   Why do it then?

KATHERINE   Perhaps because when we fight is about the only time I feel alive.

Suddenly she flinches, her hand moving about her abdomen again.

AMANDA   What is it?

KATHERINE   I'm not sure . . .

AMANDA looks up at her sister suddenly, a look of apprehension and astonishment on her face.

9   Ext. Katherine's Flat. Day.   9

The tower block, grim and windswept.

Terry's pick-up truck can be seen, about to pull out of the forecourt.

AMANDA comes breathlessly reeling out of the front entrance.

> AMANDA Terry . . . Terry!

AMANDA shouts on at him, and TERRY brakes abruptly, sticking his head out of the window.

> AMANDA You'd better come back . . . it's Katherine . . .
>   I think she's started . . .

10 Int. Amanda's Bedroom. Night. Studio. 10

AMANDA, in dressing gown and nightdress, is sitting at her dressing table, applying make-up in the mirror.

As she leans back to scrutinise the effect of the make-up, quite liberally applied, PATTI'S DISC appears to the right hand of the frame.

> PATTI Oh more, definitely. Fellas like lashings of make-up . . . and you want Gary to notice you, don't you?

As AMANDA leans forward to continue her endeavours with mascara and eye shadow, a voice from downstairs intrudes . . .

PATTI'S DISC evaporates.

> JUNE (*OOV*) Amanda! AMANDA! Do you want this
>   tea or what?

11 Int. Kitchen. Night. Studio. 11

The kitchen clock tells us it's past midnight.

The FAMILY, all dressed in pyjamas and dressing gowns, are seated around the table. A slightly tense atmosphere of waiting pervades . . .

FRANK is the only one not seated. He is quietly pacing in the background.

AMANDA enters, and moves to sit and drink her tea.

> AMANDA What's the time now?
>
> MICHAEL About fifteen minutes later than when you last asked.

AMANDA says nothing, she sips her tea. FRANK paces on.

> FRANK Maybe I should get round to the hospital . . . keep Terry company while he waits.
>
> JUNE I'm sure he'd rather be on his own, Frank.

FRANK resumes his walking. Then glances at AMANDA'S FACE.

> FRANK What on earth have you done to your face?
>
> AMANDA (*Slightly embarrassed*) Put some make-up on.
>
> FRANK At this time of night?
>
> AMANDA I was trying something out.
>
> MICHAEL You can say that again. (*Amanda kicks him under the table, which he avoids. Frank cuffs him on the head.*) I'm for bed. Give us a shout if you hear anything.

As MICHAEL passes AMANDA he hurls more insults. Real sibling horseplay, which masks something else.

For a moment, the only movement in the room is FRANK, pacing the floor.

AMANDA'S FACE, as if this thought hadn't properly registered before.

> FRANK What the hell's keeping him?

JUNE   (*Indulgently almost, to Amanda, about the pacing Frank*) He's more nervous than we are. (*To her husband*) Why don't you go up, Frank? You've work tomorrow, remember.

FRANK   (*Reluctantly*) Well, be sure and . . .

He moves towards JUNE, and she raises her cheek, for a kiss.

Instead, however, and quite unintentionally, FRANK leans down by her, to retrieve a newspaper from the table. Leaving JUNE feeling foolish and unaccountably embarrassed, feeling the eyes of her daughter upon her.

As FRANK goes, JUNE hastily rises, camouflaging the moment, and her reaction to it, in a small flurry of activity.

A pause.

AMANDA   She'll be glad when it's all over as well. (*As June glances at her*) Kath . . . she said the waiting was getting them down.

JUNE   If you feel odd about being an aunt, imagine how they do about being parents . . . they're not that much older than you, are they?

AMANDA'S FACE, digesting this. JUNE is still busy with cups and plates.

JUNE   And having babies . . . children . . . it's not always the pretty picture people like to paint . . . sometimes . . . if you're not careful, they can come between a couple.

There's the slightest change in JUNE'S TONE. We should realise she is now talking about herself, as much as KATHERINE.

The telephone starts to ring, they look at each other and spring into action.

12 Int. Hall. Night. Studio.   12

FRANK and MICHAEL, strapping on dressing gowns, running
down the stairs, two at a time.

13 Int. Sitting Room. Night. Studio.   13

JUNE and AMANDA, hurtling to the phone. JUNE picks it up.

> JUNE Hello, yes? . . . Yes, Terry? . . . (*The faces of
> the family, waiting and watching*) . . . And
> Katherine? . . . Of course . . . yes . . . (*Then*)
> No, go ahead and call them, we'll talk to you
> later.

She hangs up and turns to them all.

> JUNE A girl, seven pounds, three ounces. They're
> both doing well. He's just ringing his parents
> to tell them . . .

> MICHAEL Whey-hey . . !

MICHAEL playfully punches his FATHER, who mock stabs
him back. While this horseplay takes place, JUNE embraces
AMANDA.

A genuine moment, uniting the family. But the moment soon
passes.

FRANK quickly recovers his usual, somewhat formal,
demeanour . . .

> FRANK Yes, well. Time we got some sleep. Make sure
> you lock up, eh?

FRANK goes, followed by MICHAEL and JUNE.

AMANDA is left alone. A look of anti-climax about her.

KATHERINE is in a corner bed, the curtains drawn around her, cutting off the rest of the ward from us. We can hear it though . . . voices, footsteps, telephones.

KATHERINE herself is propped up against pillows in bed. She looks tired still, but less than she did when pregnant.

The BABY is sleeping beside her.

AMANDA is stooped over it, all agog and goggle-eyed.

> AMANDA   She's beautiful. Beautiful. Have you thought of a name yet?

> KATHERINE   Not Diana. Every other baby in here seems to be called that. The place is stiff with them.

> AMANDA   Does she always sleep like this?

> KATHERINE   Some chance. She's got a pair of lungs on her, I'll tell you.

> AMANDA   Mum and Dad are coming tonight. Dad's bringing his camera.

> KATHERINE   People always go soggy over babies. Especially men. Perhaps because they don't have to look after them.

There's something in her tone . . . a slight edge. But AMANDA is too pre-occupied with the infant to notice.

> AMANDA   What does Terry think of her?

> KATHERINE   Love at first sight. I'll be lucky to get a look in. (*Something about this remark does register with Amanda, and she glances up*) What's up?

> AMANDA   (*Slowly, hesitantly*) Just something Mum said, last night . . .

> KATHERINE   About what?

AMANDA   Having babies and stuff. How it can come
          between a couple.

We see KATHERINE'S FACE.

AMANDA   (*Stoops over the baby again*) You wouldn't come
          between anyone would you, eh? You little
          lovely, Eh? Eh?

We hold on KATHERINE'S FACE. Something reflected there.

15   Ext. Urban Area/Wall. Day.   15

Open on a wide, high, brick wall, as big as we can get.

A group of GIRLS in dungarees and overalls are putting up
ladders and trestle tables. POLLY and AMANDA are amongst
them.

First, however, we see JO, shouting instructions as the GIRLS
make a rough kind of scaffold.

While all this is going on we cut to AMANDA and POLLY.
They are crouched, along with two other girls, beside some
large pots of paint, busy stirring and mixing.

POLLY   You ought to be with the others doing the
          painting, Mandy. Anyone can do this.

AMANDA   I'd rather stop here.

POLLY   Come on . . . you're about the only person
          here who can draw a straight line, aren't you?

AMANDA   We're allowed to choose what we do, aren't
          we? I thought that was the point.

Angrily POLLY mixes the paint.

POLLY   What would you know about the point? You
          never listen, do you?

AMANDA   Says who?

POLLY You think it's just a game. It's not. If we don't make a good job of it, we don't get paid.

AMANDA Since when are you suddenly in charge?

They glare at each other. As they do, a shadow falls across them. They look up to see JO.

JO What's going on?

AMANDA (*Sullenly*) I just don't like being given orders.

POLLY I simply said she should be one of the painters, that's all.

HILARY What about it, Amanda? You're probably the best we've got . . .

AMANDA (*Throwing down her brush*) Yes, ma'am, no ma'am, three bags full ma'am!

AMANDA scrambles up, and starts to move off. But with one parting shot over her shoulder, to POLLY . . .

AMANDA (*Tartly*) Of course, you prefer the company of my brother these days, you've made that pretty obvious . . .

She goes. HILARY and POLLY exchange a look.

We cut to a wider shot.

AMANDA is now climbing one of the ladders, ready to start helping with the mural.

We cut again, to see we are watching her from someone's viewpoint.

GARY, lounging on his bike, is covertly observing her.

16 Int. Amanda's Hall. Day. Studio. 16

The doorbell is ringing. AMANDA swings downstairs to answer it.

POLLY stands there. A slightly awkward moment.

> POLLY Look Mandy I . . .

> AMANDA (*Cutting in*) Michael! For you.

And she moves abruptly away, back up the stairs, leaving POLLY open-mouthed by the open door.

17   Int. Kitchen. Early Evening. Studio.   17

FRANK, Reading the evening paper. JUNE preparing supper.

AMANDA, some school books in front of her again, is sharpening a pencil. Distractedly, allowing the curled ends of the sharpened pencil to form a long chain from the blade of the sharpener.

JUNE and FRANK exchange a look.

> JUNE I wish you'd go in there and join them,
> Amanda, instead of skulking around in here.

> AMANDA They didn't exactly ask me to, did they?

> JUNE And you didn't exactly give them a chance, did
> you?

A pause.

> FRANK (*Just a throwaway*) Friendship is like anything
> else, Amanda. You have to learn to share it . . .

AMANDA'S FACE, glancing at him.

18   Int. Amanda's Hall. Evening. Studio.   18

AMANDA, emerging from the kitchen.

She looks towards the partly-open door of the sitting room. Vaguely, we can hear the sound of pop music coming from within, and voices.

Tentatively, she prods the door open a few inches. We see
MICHAEL and POLLY, their backs to us, on the sofa. One arm
of MICHAEL's, slung over POLLY's shoulders.

As AMANDA watches, her brother pulls her friend towards
him, and kisses her.

AMANDA quickly withdraws, to run up the stairs . . .

19   Int. Amanda's bedroom. Night. Studio.   19

It's late, about one am. AMANDA can't sleep. She tosses
about in bed for a moment, before giving up. She reaches
out, to switch on a radio by the bed. And then lies back,
looking up at the pictures of POLLY and herself, illuminated
by a beam from the street light.

We hold on AMANDA'S FACE, as the radio tunes in.

We hear the professional tones of a DISC JOCKEY. He is
chairing a phone-in.

> DJ   (*OOV*) So long as you feel better having talked it
> over with someone, Tony, that's the point . . .

> TONY   (*OOV*) I do . . . definitely.

> DJ   Great. That's what it's all about. OK, coming up
> to one am. here on Problem Phone-in, the
> news in a minute, but first we've got June on
> the line . . . hello there, June . . ?

AMANDA'S FACE, only half-listening.

> JUNE   (*Distorted, OOV*) Hello . . ?

> DJ   What can we do for you then, June?

> JUNE   (*Distorted, OOV*) I don't really know where to
> start . . .

AMANDA'S FACE. Recognition dawning . . .

The hall, dark and unlit.

AMANDA emerges from her bedroom, and starts to go down the stairs. Slowly, listening as she goes. OOV, we can hear JUNE, quietly talking . . .

> JUNE (*OOV*) I've been married nearly twenty years . . . and they've been good years . . . Except now, we just don't seem to talk to each other . . . or touch each other . . .

We see AMANDA'S FACE.

We are now outside the sitting room door, once again. It is partly open.

Inside, we can see JUNE in her nightdress and dressing gown. Dishevelled, a kind of restrained distress about her . . .

AMANDA'S FACE, listening at the open door.

> JUNE . . . It's not that we don't care for each other . . . we've just got out of the habit of showing it . . . (*Amanda moves, so that she can see her mother, stooped over the telephone*) I cook the meals, clean the house . . . and he appreciates what I do, I know. He just doesn't appreciate *me*. As a person. If he doesn't respect me, if my family don't respect me, how am I supposed to respect myself?

AMANDA'S FACE, a kind of stunned confusion there.

Cut to:

Upper landing. AMANDA, *en route* back to her bedroom. She passes her parents' bedroom. There, through the door, she can see her FATHER. Noisily, obliviously asleep.

21   Int. Amanda's Bedroom. Day. Studio.   21

The following morning.

AMANDA is thoughtfully altering a jumper, looking at her reflection in the dressing table mirror. Suddenly, something beyond the window attracts her attention.

She rises. Looking out of the window she sees GARY leaving.

22   Int. Amanda's Hall. Day. Studio.   22

AMANDA picks up a message GARY has put through the letterbox. He has asked her to see him on Saturday.

PATTI'S
VOICE OVER   Now that Gary has popped the question, will Amanda say yes? . . . What is in store for Katherine and her new baby? . . . Will Michael and Polly make it together? . . . to be continued . . .

End of Episode Three

A closer look at . . .

Education

In the past classes at school were often labelled 'boys' and 'girls' subjects. When your parents were at school, Cooking, Needlework, and Child-care were for the girls, and Science, Woodwork, and Metalwork for the boys. The problem with this was that it cut down people's choices considerably. Today too, you may be discouraged from taking a particular subject that interests you because it is thought by others (including your friends) to be unsuitable.

This kind of segregated education undoubtedly limits your options in later life. What you have studied at school determines to a great extent what kind of job you get. Your future is also affected by your attitude towards yourself. If you are confident about your domestic abilities because these were the kind of classes you took at school, you will feel more inclined towards a future running a home – as many girls do. If you took more academic or job-orientated lessons, you would probably view your future as one outside the home, like many boys. A separate 'role-bound' education limits both sexes in the way they look at themselves and each other.

Since 1975 when the Sex Discrimination Act was introduced in Britain, it has been against the law for British schools to discriminate against either sex. However, some schools, like Amanda's, continue to separate boys and girls in some subjects. What happens in your school? Even if your school officially allows either sex to take any subject, do you feel pressure to go in a particular direction? Girls often feel that they ought to like Home Economics, Textiles, and Office Practice, and boys feel obliged to dismiss these subjects. Which subjects are thought of as boys' subjects? What are the pressures that cause us to think this way? Is it the school itself, or are other social factors involved? What effect do you think your schooling will have on your attitude to your future?

In academic subjects there also appears to be gender bias. Girls often prefer and do better at English, Languages, and Art; boys seem more inclined towards the Sciences and Maths. Can you think of any reasons for this?

In *S.W.A.L.K.*, Hilary and Jo are fighting for a chance to be treated and seen as equal in education. They want a free choice regardless of sex. Even if they succeed, how much choice will they *really* have? How much will parents, friends, TV, advertisements, magazines, and books pressurise them into thinking a certain way about themselves and their future?

It is interesting to speculate on what has made us the way we are now. Were you born the way you are? What have been the major influences in your life? How much are your opinions about school influenced by your parents or your friends? Are you ever truly able to decide something by yourself?

EPISODE FOUR

'Saturday Night Fever'

Synopsis

Katherine's baby is born – to a united welcome. The feminist movement at school has gathered momentum, but is threatened by sabotage from the boys. June, Amanda's mother, frustrated and feeling her family have outgrown their need for her, attempts to get a job. She discovers that while she feels she no longer has a place at home, the outside world has no place for her either.

Patti's presence has paid off and Amanda has her first date. Suddenly romance turns into sex and Amanda finds reality conflicts with the idyll which Patti promised her.

1   Ext. Urban Area. Wall. (Mural) Day.   1

Open on a pile of our romantic magazines. Some have paint pots standing on them, others are simply stacked up in piles . . . They are on a trestle table, pages fluttering in the breeze.

1A   Standard Int. Magazine Montage.   1A

As in previous episodes, the image of the magazines fills the screen . . . Hearts and flowers and speech bubbles, amorous girls and lusty lads.

And as before, voices accompany the images, trembling with tenderness, mellow with emotion.

Once again, we allow the voices to drift and bleed into one another rising in a confused crescendo.

Now we see PATTI'S FACE, beaming out at us from the Problem Page.

As the voices rise, like a crest of a wave, we abruptly cut to silence.

Super the episode title:

1B   Sub-title   1B

Bring up the episode title:

Episode Four, Saturday Night Fever.

Cut to:

1C   Ext. Urban Area. Wall. Day.   1C

The mural has considerably progressed since we last saw it.

What is actually depicted isn't important. It can be abstract or representational, but it should be reasonably impressive – extremely large and *very* colourful.

AMANDA, along with a couple of other GIRLS, is up on a ladder, painting.

Nearby, POLLY and a group of GIRLS are busy mixing paints.

JO can be seen, strutting about, organising and generally overseeing. She pauses a moment, eyes on AMANDA, who is standing, day dreaming on the top of her ladder. A flicker of irritation from JO before she speaks . . .

> JO Can we have some more black?

> POLLY Coming up.

HILARY skids up on a bike, pulling to a halt beside JO.

> JO Hey, it's really coming on, isn't it?

> HILARY (*Modestly; you'd think it was all her own work*)
> They can't say they haven't got their money's worth.

JO I've just spoken to my father . . . the council have got a do planned for when they hand over the cheque . . . The local press have all been invited.

HILARY Good, terrific. The more publicity the better.

They stand a moment, watching the girls. The atmosphere is definitely one of industrious concentration.

HILARY'S EYES rest on AMANDA.

HILARY She's pretty good, (*As Jo glances at her*) I thought she'd never actually go along with it . . . never mind do as well as that.

JO You still have to watch her though. She's got her head in the clouds half the time, that one.

Cut to AMANDA, dreamily painting.

POLLY scrambles up the ladder next to her, with a jug of mixed black paint which she pours into a pot.

AMANDA Thanks.

AMANDA starts softly humming as she paints, POLLY watches her a moment.

POLLY Mandy? (*There's something about the way she says it, as if it's important to her*) Michael and I are going up to town on Saturday night. Do you fancy coming along?

AMANDA As it happens . . . I've got a date.

POLLY freezes, all interest suddenly.

POLLY Who with?

HILARY (*Calling from below*) Polly! More of the green needed over here.

POLLY Be right there! (*To Amanda, in a hissed whisper*) Who . . ? come on!

111

AMANDA   You'd better go.

And with this reply, AMANDA turns back to the mural,
humming once again.

POLLY'S FACE, grimacing slightly, before she goes.

2   Ext. Fashion Boutique. Day.   2

A teenage-fashion boutique, all coloured canopies and
thudding rock music emanating from within.

AMANDA is window-shopping, looking at the mannequins
in the various garments. She looks at one in particular. A
blue kind of track suit effort.

Cut to:

2A   Fantasy Sequence.   2A

We are now into photographic effects once more. We see
AMANDA, but this time a still. She is wearing the blue outfit,
and is draped decoratively by her front door, greeting GARY.

AMANDA   (*All seductive and cat-like*)
Hi, Gary . . . glad you could make it . . .

Cut back to:

2B   Ext. Fashion Boutique. Day.   2B

Real time.

AMANDA, outside the boutique. She turns to look at another
outfit.

A yellow top with a matching skirt.

Cut to:

Fantasy sequence. Photographic stills. AMANDA, in a different pose from before. Once again, greeting GARY by her front door.

AMANDA 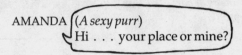 (*A sexy purr*)
Hi . . . your place or mine?

Cut back to AMANDA . . . and real time again.

2D   Ext. Fashion Boutique. Day.   2D

Outside the boutique once more. AMANDA's eyes move on to a dress.

Cut to:

Real time.

Noises from the street and cars pervade her reverie. AMANDA enters the boutique.

We move in, to see the blue outfit on the first mannequin.

Hold on that image and cut to:

3   Int. Katherine's Bedroom. Day. Studio.   3

The blue outfit, now in KATHERINE's hands, as she holds it against herself, studying herself in the wardrobe mirror.

She is wearing one of TERRY's shirts over jeans. Hair uncombed, face free of make-up.

We pull out, to see the room.

Baby blankets, shawls, nappies, a changing-mat strewn liberally about. OOV, we can hear the BABY herself, crying fit to bust.

KATHERINE   (*Matter-of factly*) It looks terrible. And so do I.
             (*She drops the outfit onto the bed*) For your date
             with thingy is it?

AMANDA   (*Slightly embarrassed, silly girl*) Gary, yes.

KATHERINE   (*Glancing at her*) It's your first time, isn't it?
             Out with a boy?

AMANDA   So?

KATHERINE   So good luck to you. You've been day dreaming
             about it long enough. Maybe it's time you put
             it to the test.

AMANDA   (*Puzzled*) Test?

KATHERINE   What a first date's all about . . . testing each
             other out . . . seeing how far you can go.

AMANDA'S FACE, this thought somehow hasn't occurred.

KATHERINE moves to sit on the bed. The outfit in her hands.
As she talks, she strokes it, as if remembering times past but
not forgotten.

KATHERINE   I first met Terry at a party. A Christmas party.
             I was just turned seventeen. He was there with
             some mates and he asked me to dance. (*A smile*)
             And that was it. He didn't lay a finger on me,
             either (*Amanda's face here*) Never even touched
             me. I was beginning to think there was
             something wrong with me. The next night,
             when he took me home, he kissed me. I'd
             never been kissed like that before, Oh boy.
             I didn't know whether to stay put and enjoy
             it or run for my life.

AMANDA   (*Curiously*) What did you do?

KATHERINE   (*A grin*) Stayed put, didn't I?

*The baby's screams reach fever pitch OOV. Drearily KATHERINE
rises.*

KATHERINE   (*Just a throw-away*) Maybe I should have cut and
run, while I had the chance.

She exits.

We move in on AMANDA'S FACE. Something slightly
apprehensive reflected there.

4   Int. Amanda's Kitchen. Day. Studio.   4

The FAMILY, sitting eating supper. Just the sound of their
munching, and the cutlery, rattling on plates.

We are on AMANDA'S FACE. She is watching her MOTHER
and FATHER, a slightly anxious curiosity about her as she
does so.

FRANK is reading the paper, propped up beside his plate.

JUNE, sitting next to him, is apparently intent on eating. Yet
there is a look about her too. Something preoccupied,
pensive.

AMANDA now turns, to glance at MICHAEL. He is wearing a
pair of headphones, attached to a radio clipped onto his
waist. Occasionally his head jigs this way and that, to the
music, inaudible of course to us, but not him.

After a long moment of silence and munching, FRANK turns
the paper over. A gaping hole in the back page greets him.

JUNE   (*Quickly*) It was me, love. There was an ad I
wanted to tear out.

FRANK   Did you have to take half my football page with
it. (*He starts to read again, a kind of vague
afterthought*) What kind of ad anyway?

JUNE   (*A beat*) For a job.

FRANK looks up at her.

115

> JUNE   A secretarial job, part time. Down at Gibson's Engineering.

> FRANK   Who's this job supposed to be for?

> JUNE   (*Quietly*) Me.

AMANDA'S FACE, watching the interplay between her parents.

In fact, we should remain on her face, her reactions, for most of the scene. We are witnessing it from her viewpoint, seeing, as it were, her parents from a new, slightly more adult viewpoint, which is the characteristic of emerging adolescence . . . Remember it – that dawning, disconcerting realisation that your parents are human too – that they are fallible, even vulnerable?

MICHAEL however, is blissfully ignorant of all this, as he mutely jogs and jigs to his canned music.

FRANK is looking at JUNE, who decides she should elaborate.

> JUNE   Why not? With you and the children out all day . . . I have to fill the time somehow don't I? (*Then, deliberately casual*) I've an interview tomorrow actually.

> FRANK   (*Sour, but only mildly so, more resigned really*) I suppose you'd have told me about it then, would you?

> JUNE   (*reasonably*) I'm telling you now, Frank.

> FRANK   Somewhat after the event.

AMANDA'S FACE once again, watching, Wimbledon-like, as her PARENTS continue.

> FRANK   But then I should be used to my family keeping me in the dark by now.

> JUNE   Frank . . . you don't mind if I take a job, surely?

116

FRANK   If it'll make you happy.

JUNE   (*Abruptly*) It won't. (*Frank and Amanda look at her in surprise*) It might, perhaps, make me feel useful.

FRANK   (*A glance at Amanda*) Don't let's go off on that one again.

A pause. Broken only by the faint sound of distorted pop music, coming from MICHAEL's head-phones.

JUNE   You say you want to be consulted about these things and when you are, you dismiss them.

FRANK   I don't want to see *you* dismissed, do I? You haven't worked for what . . . nineteen years is it? You're out of touch . . . Besides which they'll want someone young, won't they?

JUNE rises with the plates. Her manner stiff, splintered with resentment.

JUNE   Thanks for the vote of confidence.

FRANK   Look, if you want to go out into the world again, you'll have to learn how to take the knocks, along with the rest of us.

JUNE   (*A beat*) It seems I can get quite enough of those without stepping outside my front door.

JUNE moves to the sink.

AMANDA'S FACE again, looking from one parent to the other. And then at MICHAEL, obliviously, heedlessly, munching and nodding to his music.

5   Int. Amanda's Hall. Night. Studio.   5

JUNE, bolting the front door, slipping the chain on.

She turns, to see AMANDA in nightdress and dressing gown, on the stairs behind her.

> AMANDA Mum? I was wondering . . . what time is your interview tomorrow?

> JUNE Four-thirty, why?

> AMANDA I . . . I could come along if you like. After school. Be a bit of moral support.

JUNE looks at her daughter a moment, as if seeing an adult there, for the first time.

> JUNE I'd like that very much, Amanda. Thank you.

AMANDA smiles, and JUNE, slightly moved, but oddly embarrassed at the same time, glances away.

Cut to:

FRANK, standing in the sitting room doorway. Newspaper under arm, a cup of tea in hand, clearly *en route* for bed.

Equally clearly, he has overheard the interchange between AMANDA and JUNE. Something remorseful in his face perhaps?

6 Ext. School. Day.   6

Just a brief establishing shot of the school, taken perhaps, when filming for episode one.

Swiftly cut to:

7 Ext. Bicycle Shed. Day.   7

Rows of bikes, stacked in their racks.

A group of BOYS are straddled about, on handlebars and saddles. They are smoking.

There are four boys present. GARY is one of them. The other three lads are aged around sixteen to seventeen. Their names, respectively, are ROSS, DOMMY and MICK.

GARY I still say it's a lousy idea.

ROSS Be a giggle though.

GARY Not if we get caught.

ROSS You worry too much.

DOMMY We'll need a fair zap of the old aerosol, it's a pretty big wall.

MICK All taken care of my son. (*He unstraps a saddle bag. Stuffed inside are several cans of aerosol spray*) A touch of el-blacko I thought. Do the job a treat.

GARY I just don't see the point.

ROSS There is no point, mate. It's a laugh, right? A thrill. But it's something to do on a Saturday night isn't it?

DOMMY Have to be after dark, to be on the safe side.

MICK So we'll take a flash.

ROSS (*To Gary*) Are you in, or what?

GARY opens his mouth to reply, but is abruptly curtailed.

MICK . . . someone's coming!

Hastily they scrabble about, to collect their bikes. In their haste, however, the saddle bags containing the aerosol sprays flap open, and the cans spill out, rolling hither and thither.

The BOYS ferret about on all fours, to retrieve them. They are thus engaged, when AMANDA enters.

Quickly the BOYS stand up, waving aside cigarette smoke, stuffing the spray cans back into the saddle bags.

> ROSS   Well lads, time we weren't here.

They start to haul out their bikes. AMANDA stands, eyes on GARY, slightly embarrassed.

The BOYS troop past her, whistling with an innocent kind of refrain . . .

GARY pauses beside her, waits for the boys to get out of earshot.

> GARY   Hi.

> AMANDA   Hello.

> GARY   (*He shuffles about slightly awkwardly*) You er . . . got my note then?

> AMANDA   Yes.

> GARY   And it's alright is it? For Saturday?

> AMANDA   Fine, smashing.

> GARY   Right then.

More shuffling, and toe scratching in the ground.

> AMANDA   So er . . . where will we go?

> GARY   Wherever you like . . . (Then, *realising he should take some initiative in the proceedings*) How about the cinema?

> AMANDA   Great. Lovely.

> GARY   Right then.

Another sticky silence. They steal a look at each other, briefly smile, and return to their shuffling.

> GARY   I'll er . . . find out what's on, see what grabs us . . . (*Pause*) Pick you up about seven OK?.

AMANDA OK . . .

GARY Right then.

They hover, uncertainly, unsure of whether the conversation is finished; apparently it is.

GARY pushes his bike past her, out of the shed. AMANDA stands, watching him go, all ecstasy and dewy-eyed.

Then her glance rests on something else.

On the ground is a tin of the aerosol spray . . .

She picks it up curiously, idly examining it a moment, before placing it on a shelf by the window. And then she goes. We remain on the aerosol spray. An ominous emphasis if you like, of things to come.

8   Int. Amanda's Hall. Day. Studio.   8

JUNE, smartly attired in a suit, is examining herself in the hall mirror, applying make-up, in readiness for her interview.

AMANDA sits on the stairs behind her, watching.

JUNE I feel quite nervous. Ridiculous, isn't it?

AMANDA (*Curiously*) Why do you want to get a job suddenly, Mum? Do we need the money?

JUNE It'll be handy, won't it? We'd better be going. Won't do much for my chances if I'm late, will it?

They are about to move to the front door, when the sound of the key alerts them. The door swings open, to reveal FRANK . . . dressed for work, a small package in one hand.

JUNE Frank . . .

FRANK Got through my round early. (*Pause*) Off for your interview are you?

JUNE   (*A beat*) That's the idea.

FRANK   (*Tossing the package over*) Something to help you
          on your way.

JUNE looks down at the packet, and back at FRANK a
moment, before she starts to tear at the wrapping, almost
child-like in her excitement to get it open.

And once again, we view the scene entirely from AMANDA's
viewpoint. The parcel contains a small, quite expensive bottle
of perfume.

JUNE   Frank!

Delighted, she turns back to the mirror liberally spraying herself.

FRANK   Go easy, or you'll asphixiate them.

JUNE   I can't help but get the job now, can I?

FRANK   It'll be a push-over, right Amanda?

AMANDA   Right.

JUNE pauses, her eyes on FRANK, in the mirror. She smiles at
him in the glass, and he returns the smile. A real tenderness
there.

We return to AMANDA'S FACE, watching.

JUNE gathers together her coat and bag, kisses FRANK
hurriedly, and moves to the front door. AMANDA follows,
but at the door she pauses, to turn back and look at her
father.

AMANDA   Dad? (*Frank, about to enter the kitchen, pauses*)
          See you.

Before he asks for elaboration, she follows her mother out.

Hold on FRANK'S FACE.

All whitewash and filing cabinets. Desks strewn with
invoices and ledgers. Distantly we can hear the sound of
typewriters pounding, telephones ringing.

Seated inconspicuously in a corner, partly obscured by a
filing cabinet, is AMANDA. One of her romantic strip
magazines inevitably on lap.

At one of the desks (there are two in the room), is a
SECRETARY. She does not speak during the action. She is
aged about nineteen, heavily intent on her typing,
manicured, painted nails flying expertly over the keys.

At the other desk, handbag nervously propped on lap, is
JUNE. She is being interviewed by another WOMAN aged
about thirty-three. Like the typist, she is immaculately
turned out. All jangling charm bracelets and flawless make-
up. Rather too much of it perhaps. A kind of tireless
professional efficiency about her.

The WOMAN is taking down June's details in shorthand. Her
manner should suggest someone who has done this before,
and repetition has long since made the job tedious, not to say
tiresome.

    WOMAN And your last employer?

    JUNE Reid Electrics.

Once again, the scene is shot from AMANDA's point of view.
She glances, now from her mother, to those fingers, darting
over typewriter keys, and back, to the tense-faced June.

JUNE looks like she's facing a firing squad.

    WOMAN Date of leaving?

    JUNE Er . . . January I think.

    WOMAN (*As she writes*) January – nineteen-eighty-two.

    JUNE Sixty-two.

*The WOMAN looks at her sharply. AMANDA winces, on her
mother's behalf.*

>WOMAN *1962?*

>>JUNE Yes . . . I've been bringing up my family you
>>see.

*AMANDA, acutely embarrassed for her mother, looks down at the
magazine on her lap in confusion.*

9A Fantasy. Hospital. 9A

There is a photo-style strip-cartoon there.

We move in on it . . .

A GIRL is lying in a hospital bed, holding a BABY in her arms.
Her handsome HUSBAND hovers over her . . .

The camera moves over the page allowing us glimpses of the
cartoon story.

>GIRL Oh Pete, this is the happiest day of my life . . .

>BOY I was afraid you might have regrets . . . giving
>up your job as an air hostess . . . all that
>travel and excitement . . .

>GIRL I can get all the excitement I need at home,
>can't I?

A close-up of her now, gazing in her baby's eyes.

>GIRL Besides, I've got a job now haven't I? The only
>one I'll ever need . . .

Towards the end of this sequence, the WOMAN'S VOICE starts to pervade AMANDA's reverie.

9B   Int. Office. Day. Studio.   9B

AMANDA glances up, back in the real world again.

> JUNE   A . . . typing test?

> WOMAN   Company policy . . . Let's get started, shall we?

The WOMAN rises, jangling charm-bracelets and silk efficiency.

Once again, AMANDA'S FACE, tensely watching.

> WOMAN   A little copy typing I think . . . just type what's on here would you?

She hands JUNE a paper with typing on it. JUNE squares herself, her hands hovering over the typewriter keys.

AMANDA'S FACE, still watching.

JUNE hesitates, glancing at the WOMAN.

> JUNE   I've not used an electric one.

> WOMAN   Most offices are electric these days.

Once again JUNE returns to the typewriter. She turns it on and it starts humming menacingly. Slowly, cautiously, she starts to type, recoiling in surprise as the carriage electrically-powered of course, noisily catapults back into position.

AMANDA flinches, and glances at the WOMAN'S FACE. The WOMAN stands, expressionlessly, like someone who has had their attention diverted from the significant to the trivial.

Painstakingly and painfully, JUNE labours on.

After a moment she hits two keys together, and all of them fly up, to jam in the top of the typewriter. The hum of the machine alters to a plaintive whine. JUNE, desperately, hits one key after another in an effort to unblock the wretched thing.

The WOMAN simply stands, as if watching a fly squirming in a spider's web.

AMANDA closes her eyes in despair.

On her shuttered eyes, cut to:

10   Int. Amanda's Kitchen. Day. Studio.   10

FRANK is making himself a cup of coffee. Sounds, OOV, cause him to stir and look towards the door.

AMANDA enters.

> FRANK Well?

> AMANDA No luck.

She stops quickly, for JUNE is entering.

JUNE looks hot and flustered from her ordeal, and contrives to look neither at FRANK nor her daughter as she reaches for a pinafore, which she straps around her waist.

FRANK and AMANDA exchange a look, uncertain as to what, if anything, they should say.

But JUNE herself, solves the problem. Her tone is brusque and business-like, defying sympathy or solace.

> JUNE Right, well. I expect you're ready for your tea?
>   (*She moves towards the kitchen area*) At least I
>   don't have to pass a test to do that.

AMANDA'S FACE once again, watching her MOTHER take up her familiar position at the sink.

AMANDA in bed.

The room is illuminated by her bedside light. She is idly flicking through one of her magazines. She pauses, a far-away look in her eyes.

We take a shot of the magazine.

11A   Fantasy.   11A

We mix to a fantasy sequence composed of photographs.

AMANDA and GARY, arm in arm. AMANDA is dressed in her blue outfit. They are coming out of a cinema.

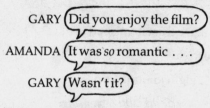

    GARY   Did you enjoy the film?

    AMANDA   It was *so* romantic . . .

    GARY   Wasn't it?

And they set off, arm in arm, down the street.

Cut to:

Still with photographic effects. We are now in a setting by a lake in a park. It is night, and shrouded in darkness.

GARY is gazing into AMANDA'S EYES. And she, as you might expect, is gazing up into his . . .

    GARY   Mind you, real life can be pretty romantic as well.

As he moves to kiss her:

AMANDA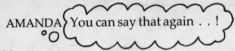

Cut to:

12   Ext. Mural. Day.   12

The mural is progressing well. AMANDA is present, up on a ladder busy painting, along with another GIRL. However, we should note that there are several girls less than before.

JO, HILARY, and POLLY, are bent over the trestle table, looking at the plan of the mural.

HILARY Just this last section to do and we're home and dry.

POLLY You think we'll get it finished in time?

JO We have to.

HILARY We'll look right idiots if we don't.

HILARY straightens up, to look at the GIRLS painting.

HILARY A pretty pathetic turn-out isn't it?

JO (*Just a throwaway*) It's a Saturday, isn't it? Everyone's busy making plans for tonight.

On the line, cut to:

The boys – ROSS, DOMMY and MICK – are crouched nearby, carefully concealed, watching the girls.

GARY cycles up, and crouches down next to them.

ROSS What kept you?

GARY I got held up . . . (*Pause*) Look . . . you'd better count me out tonight, fellas (*Mick, Dommy and Ross exchange a glance*) I'm busy.

DOMMY Oh sure.

ROSS We get the message.

GARY I am. I've got . . . something on. I can't break it even if I wanted to.

ROSS (*Tartly*) Which you don't want to, right?

GARY is clearly in a no win situation. Since he can't think of a reply he goes, clambers onto his bike, and rides off. ROSS resumes looking at the mural.

A close-up of paint being applied to the wall. The brush, passing over the rugged surface, coating it in colour.

Cut to:

13   Int. Amanda's Bedroom. Evening. Studio.   13

A close-up of more paint being applied.

This time on AMANDA'S FACE. She is at the dressing table, preparing for her date.

We pull out, as she regards her reflection, squinting so as to get a better impression. She certainly hasn't spared on the glitter effect make-up or the lip gloss. Her hair is crimped for the occasion.

She is totally absorbed in the job, giving it all she's got. As she concentrates PATTI'S DISC appears, right of frame. All beams and benevolence again.

PATTI That's the idea . . . a bit more of the blusher I think . . ? And remember, take advice from an old hand . . . it's not what you say, it's how you look, that's what counts. So don't try and impress him with your mind, no clever stuff, right? Just agree with whatever he says and look pretty. It's the only way, believe me.

The door bell rings, OOV, and the disc evaporates. Hastily, AMANDA rises, runs to her door.

14   Int. Amanda's Hall. Evening. Studio.   14

MICHAEL, getting the front door. To see POLLY standing there. Unlike AMANDA, she isn't dolled up – simply dressed in jeans and a T-shirt, with a modest amount of make-up.

AMANDA watches from the top of the stairs, as the scene ensues.

> POLLY All set?

> MICHAEL Just get my jacket. (*Calling as he does*) See you later, Mum!

> JUNE (*OOV*) Not too late, Michael remember.

> MICHAEL About midnight, OK? (*He turns to Polly*) What time's your check-in?

> POLLY (*A face*) Eleven-thirty.

> MICHAEL Better get this show on the road then.

He slings an arm around her, and she around him. And they go, banging the front door shut behind them.

We return to AMANDA, watching from her hiding place.

15   Int. Amanda's Bedroom. Evening. Studio.   15

AMANDA enters her room, leaning against the door.

PATTI'S DISC appears once again.

> PATTI Come on, now . . . it'll work out for you too. How about some more lip gloss while you're at it?

As AMANDA moves dutifully to obey, cut to:

16   Int. Katherine's Bedroom. Night. Studio.   16

KATHERINE, lying on the rumpled bed, reading Dr Spock.
The room is still littered with baby gear. TERRY is putting on
his shirt on the other side of the room.

>TERRY   (*Buttoning up a shirt, looking at himself in the
>mirror*) Saturday nights. Used to be the
>highlight of our week, remember?

KATHERINE puts down the book.

>KATHERINE   I was thinking the same thing.

He moves, to sit on the bed beside her, and takes her hand.

>TERRY   You don't regret any of it, do you?

*And he says it like he's been meaning to ask this question for some
time, but rather dreads the answer.*

>KATHERINE   What?

>TERRY   . . . Getting ourselves lumbered the way we
>did.

>KATHERINE   I wish we'd thought it through a bit more, . . .
>about what was involved. I mean, a year ago
>we'd be getting ready for a Saturday night
>out ourselves wouldn't we?

TERRY caresses her hand a moment.

>TERRY   We'll have fun again, you'll see.

Hold on KATHERINE'S FACE.

17   Int. Amanda's Sitting Room. Day. Studio   17

AMANDA'S FACE, made up to the nines, but it doesn't mask
her nerves. She is sitting on the sofa, nervously twining her
handbag strap between her fingers, eyes on the mantle clock.

JUNE is sitting in an armchair, knitting a baby garment. FRANK is at a table by the window, making some kind of model aeroplane. Both parents glance at one another, clearly dismayed at AMANDA's obvious appearance. Perhaps the television is quietly playing.

Then suddenly, the door bell rings. AMANDA rises swiftly, almost tripping over in her haste to get to the door.

> AMANDA See you later then.

> > JUNE Bye, love . . . not too late mind.

18 Int. Hall. Day.   18

AMANDA, moving to the front door. Before opening it she pauses, bracing herself slightly. Allowing a smile of greeting to form on her lips.

She opens the door.

> AMANDA (*A beat*) Hi.

> > GARY Hi. Sorry I'm late. The busses, you know.

> AMANDA It's OK.

She beams at him and they exit.

19 Int. Amanda's Sitting Room. Day.   19

FRANK drops the curtain and turns back to JUNE.

> > JUNE What's he like?

> > FRANK Surprisingly presentable. Let's just hope he doesn't get any ideas.

JUNE looks rather startled.

> > FRANK Dressed the way she is, what lad wouldn't?

JUNE's face, as if this thought hadn't occurred to her.

A noisy, windswept street corner.

AMANDA's hair is billowing in the wind. Traffic roars noisily by.

AMANDA and GARY are pausing uncertainly, his hands stuck deep into pocket.

> AMANDA   What's the plan then?
>
> GARY   Eh?
>
> AMANDA   Where are we going?
>
> GARY   Depends. What do you fancy?
>
> AMANDA   I thought you said the cinema? (*His face, slightly vacant*) You said you'd find out what was on and . . .
>
> GARY   Oh well. We'll take a look shall we? See what grabs us.

They start to tramp off, but in different directions. AMANDA pauses.

> AMANDA   Gary? (*Pause*) I thought we were going to the cinema?
>
> GARY   We are.
>
> AMANDA   (*The faintest splinter of impatience there*) It's this way, isn't it?
>
> GARY   Oh. Right.

They set off once again.

A wide shot. The warm and welcoming lights from the foyer.

But a cold unwelcoming sign outside: FULL UP.

GARY and AMANDA dither a moment before moving off. As they do so AMANDA catches her heeled shoe in the cracks of the pavement. The heel and shoe part company.

> AMANDA Oh no!!

She bends to retrieve the heel, tugs it out, and stands again . . . AMANDA'S FACE, looking down at the wrecked shoe. This isn't how she planned it at all.

22   Ext. River. Night.   22

Some kind of towpath by the water.

We can see AMANDA and GARY walking along it. Not arm in arm, for AMANDA's ungainly hobbling, thanks to her heelless shoe, prevents this.

But there isn't what you'd call romance there either.

GARY is talking. AMANDA is idly listening as she limps along, her jacket pulled tightly around her.

> GARY   . . . Fly fishing's the best . . . that's where the
> skill is . . . have to have a decent rod and that.
> And know where to go. Some places are
> useless. Too much pollution, not to mention
> the river craft . . . frighten the fish off before
> you've even seen 'em.

AMANDA'S FACE, stifling a yawn.

23   Ext. River. Night.   23

GARY and AMANDA, she still plodding lopsidedly alongside him.

GARY still talking . . . arms outstretched.

GARY   . . . Didn't half put up a fight as I reeled it in . . . you should have seen it. And the weight of it! Must have been at least . . .

AMANDA   (*Abruptly*) I'm cold.

GARY   Sorry?

AMANDA   And hungry.

GARY   No hurry is there?

AMANDA   Not if we want to freeze to death.

GARY'S FACE. Now we realise his chat and indecision have been due to exactly the same nerves as she is suffering from.

GARY   Put my jacket on if you like.

AMANDA'S FACE: Now this is more like it – a chivalrous act at last.

He starts to tug off his windcheater, but in doing so, manages to spill the loose change out of the pockets.

They both bend to retrieve it, and crash their heads together in the process. AMANDA reels back slightly, holding her forehead.

GARY   Sorry . . . are you OK?

AMANDA   Just about.

She hobbles over to a bench, nearby. He follows, placing the jacket around her shoulders.

So they sit, she on one end of the bench, him on the other.

And then silence. Just the sound of the water and the night and their breathing. They steal a look at one another, and hastily glance away.

Clearly something should happen, but what? And who starts it?

GARY clears his throat.

GARY   Warming up?

AMANDA   A bit. (*Pause*) Thank you.

Another pause.

GARY shifts his position, slides nearer her. One arm, casually resting on the back of the bench. Moving slowly towards her.

AMANDA freezes slightly, as contact is finally made. Assuming this an encouraging sign, GARY continues. Nuzzling up to her, bringing his other hand into action, caressing her.

AMANDA   (*Uncertainly*) Gary . . . ?

GARY'S FACE is now buried somewhere in her neck.

GARY   I need warming up too, don't I?

His hands start to move to her buttons and her breasts. She looks down in alarm.

AMANDA   Gary . . .

GARY   Don't worry . . .

A small struggle ensues, while he vainly soldiers on.

AMANDA   *No!*

He pulls back to his own side of the bench.

GARY   You don't have to make a great drama out of it.

Silence.

AMANDA   I thought we were going somewhere nice. Not freeze out here all evening.

GARY   If I'd coughed up on some cinema tickets it would be alright would it?

AMANDA   That–is–not–what–I–said!

He's cross because he has been rejected and she is because . . . well, because of a lot of crushed hopes and dreams.

They continue to sit, in confused and angry silence.

PATTI'S DISC appears, to the right of Amanda's head.

PATTI   Amanda? . . . Cool it. He only wants to be friendly doesn't he? After all, you don't want your best friend and brother outshining you, do you?

AMANDA   Oh . . .

PATTI'S DISC evaporates.

GARY   (*In surprise*) Eh?

AMANDA   I . . . I think I'd better go.

She rises, struggling out of his jacket.

GARY   It's early yet.

AMANDA   Sorry. I think it's best. (*She hands him back the jacket*) I just don't see how you could . . . before even knowing someone.

GARY   Gawd.

AMANDA   I'm sorry, I don't.

GARY   It's a way of getting to know someone, isn't it?

AMANDA   There are other ways, aren't there?

AMANDA marches off.

GARY'S FACE, ruefully watching. Before rising, to walk off in the opposite direction.

AMANDA hobbling across the car-park towards the mural.

She sees the mural. It is stained and scarred with black spray-on graffiti.

GIRLS SHOULD BE SEEN AND NOT HEARD

EQUAL RIGHTS MEANS EQUAL BRAINS

GIRLS ARE STUPID

And so on.

AMANDA looks at it and a sob catches her. A sob of anger, frustration and sheer confusion. She glances down, to see one of the aerosol sprays.

Sobbing openly now, she picks it up and is about to hurl it away, when she recognises it.

She looks at the wall again . . . realisation dawning.

And then, beside herself with anger, she marches up to the wall. Angrily, half-crying, she starts to try and spray out the boy's words. The black paint spilling over her hands and blue outfit. But she is clearly beyond caring.

We hear footsteps behind her. Terrified, she spins around. A POLICEMAN stands there. Taking in the tear-stained face, the paint-stained overalls.

Freeze.

PATTIS'
VOICE OVER   How will Amanda get out of this one?

Will she and Gary *ever* get it together?

Is her friendship with Polly really on the rocks?

To be continued . . . next week.

End of Episode Four

A closer look at . . .

Sexual relationships

Making relationships with others seems to be a basic human activity, and sexual attraction is part of some relationships. When we first meet someone we like we make an effort to get to know them. Getting to know someone and learning to trust them takes time. Relationships develop and often improve as we begin to understand what the other person is really like. Should the sexual aspect of a relationship progress in a similar way? We would not tell someone we hardly know all our personal thoughts and secrets. Getting to know someone physically and sexually is much the same as understanding them as a friend. If you like each other all aspects of a relationship will improve with time and knowledge.

A friendship which involves sexual attraction can progress through varying degrees of intimacy. If you find someone attractive it does not mean you need automatically be thinking in terms of sexual intercourse. You can show love and affection in lots of ways – like kissing, touching, and hugging.

Showing love for one another, and having sex, should be happy, friendly and caring. It is, however, all too often an experience riddled with fears, doubt, and guilt. Why do you think this is? Think about the attitudes of the people around you towards sex. You will probably be aware of the variety of attitudes and opinions expressed by parents, friends, and by people on television and in the newspapers. What effect has the emergence of the AIDS virus had on your attitudes towards sexual relationships? Do you think it will change people's attitudes and behaviour? You need to think carefully about what you believe to be right and wrong for you.

When thinking about and discussing sexual relationships the question of contraception arises. Where can young people find out about reliable and effective forms of contraception? Why do so many young girls like Katherine become pregnant before they want to? Is it just a matter of saying, 'It's alright, it won't happen to me,' or 'We'll try and be careful'? What does this last statement mean when people are not using an effective method of birth control? How has the spread of AIDS affected people's choice of contraception? Who are the people around you who you could trust to be sympathetic and give sound advice? Is it friends, parents, or maybe a teacher that you like?

The most important thing to think about when considering birth control is the relationship itself. Should preventing an unwanted pregnancy be a shared responsibility? It takes two people to make a baby. If two people find that they are unable to discuss this in a relaxed and serious way, then maybe they are not close enough or good enough friends to have sex. How well should you know someone, and what kind of feelings should you have for them before you think of having sex?

Amanda, when preparing for her date, concerns herself totally with her physical appearance. She convinces herself that this is her most important asset. She tries to make herself physically attractive to Gary and yet seems surprised and offended when he tries to touch her. Why is this? What did she want the date to be like? Does Gary touch her because he feels that this is what is expected of him? Magazines, advertisements, and pop songs often encourage us to think like this. Have you ever thought of the consequences of this way of thinking? How does it affect the way others think of us and behave towards us? What does it say about the way we think about ourselves?

EPISODE FIVE

'Dem Old Dreams
are only in your Head'

Synopsis

Amanda's conflict with Patti and her disastrous date persists.
At school there is a confusion about who sabotaged the
feminist mural. Wherever Amanda looks she can see only
despair . . . Katherine, marooned in her high rise flat . . .
her mother, trapped in her respectable semi . . . her father
trying to keep his boyhood dreams alive. And the
whispering, cajolling Patti continues to taunt her. Can the
futility of the dreams she promises turn Amanda's despair
into a new determination?

1   Int. Toilet. Amanda's School. Day.   1

As before, the first images which fill the screen are those
from the teenage magazines.

More true-to-life soap operas, pop stars and Problem
Pages . . .

1A   Standard Int. Magazine Montage.   1A

The pages of the magazine are being idly turned. As they are,
once again, those voices build, OOV.

The magazine now turns to reveal Patti's Problem Page.

Once again, the voices build, OOV.

Bring up the episode title:

Episode Five, 'Dem Old Dreams are only in your Head'.

1C   Int. Girls Toilet. Day. Film.   1C

We pull back to see that we are inside the girls' toilets at the school. Graffiti-stained walls and grubby basins.

We now see it was a fourteen year-old GIRL who was reading the magazine, idly flicking through it while waiting for her FRIEND to wash her hands.

They start to thread their way out of the toilets, passing JO, HILARY and POLLY as they do.

The three of them are talking, vaguely checking their appearance in the mirror.

> JO   (*As if in answer to one of the others*) She was caught in the act, wasn't she? What more proof do you want?

> POLLY   I don't believe it.

> HILARY   You don't want to, you mean.

> JO   Who's she got to see?

> HILARY   Deputy head.

> JO   (*Venomously*) Well she deserves everything she gets.

> POLLY   But why – why would she do it?

> JO   She never wanted to go along with it in the first place, did she?

> POLLY   But she *did* go along with it, didn't she? She worked as hard as anyone.

JO   When she wasn't day dreaming, which was most of the time.

POLLY   Well I still don't believe it. What reason could she have?

JO   It's obvious . . . someone put her up to it didn't they? Probably that boy she had a date with. (*Polly's face*) Face it, she's the type.

HILARY   Face it, she's the type who'll do anything to please. Just like she went along with us when she wasn't even interested, so she went along with him. I'll lay odds that's what happened. I tell you, she'll blow with whatever wind happens to be passing, that one.

POLLY'S FACE again, torn by the logic of Jo's words, and her own loyalty to Amanda.

JO glances at her, as if sensing her dilemma.

JO   She's right, Polly. You can see her kind everywhere. Faceless, mindless girls with their heads stuck in those trashy magazines . . . They can't see they're being conned, they can't see anything except getting a boyfriend and getting married. It's pathetic.

HILARY   (*Bluntly*) And so is she. We've wasted our time on her long enough.

JO exits, followed by HILARY. POLLY is about to follow, when the sound of one of the toilet doors opening causes her to pause.

AMANDA emerges.

For a second the two girls stand, their eyes held across the room. Before POLLY averts hers and hastily exits.

AMANDA, in a dreary, desultory kind of way moves towards the mirror. And the face that greets her has a stark despair about it . . .

VOICE OOV I'm waiting, Amanda . . .

Cut to

2 Int. Miss Sullivan's Careers Office. Day. 2 Studio.

We open on the face of the DEPUTY HEAD. A woman in her mid-thirties. An abrasive woman, toughened perhaps by her experiences in a large comprehensive, but still young enough to recall something of the confusion of youth.

She is squarely confronting AMANDA in the empty classroom. Clearly she has decided on a brusque, head-on approach to the incident. Yet she is perplexed by the incident, and AMANDA's attitude to it.

AMANDA stands, eyes lowered, she seems defeated somehow, dispirited, as if lacking the armour to defend herself.

The teacher, MISS SULLIVAN, waits, then gives a small gesture of impatience. But she matches AMANDA's silence, and in the yawning pause, we can hear the sounds of the school beyond.

MISS
SULLIVAN Well?

AMANDA (*Dully*) I haven't got anything to say.

MISS
SULLIVAN You're not going to be very popular, you do realise that? Your parents, your friends, they're not going to think much of you after this, are they?

AMANDA (*That dull, defeated tone*) They didn't before.

MISS SULLIVAN pauses in her pacing to look at her curiously.

MISS
SULLIVAN   What does that mean? (*But Amanda clearly
regrets speaking and resumes her dogged
silence*) You're not leaving me much choice,
are you? I can't let it go you know, Amanda.
It was a stupid, destructive act and I'm tired of
repeating myself about this sort of thing. (*She
waits, as if hoping this might provoke some
response*) I'm going to give you one last
opportunity to say something about it . . .
explain what happened.

*AMANDA glances at her, and opens her mouth, as if to speak. But
seems to think better of it, and snaps her mouth closed again.*

MISS
SULLIVAN   Don't you care what happens to you?

AMANDA   Not especially.

MISS
SULLIVAN   Then I've no alternative. Warnings obviously
don't work so I'm going to have to get tough.
Perhaps then the message will get through.
(*Pause*) You're suspended for one week.

Shot of AMANDA'S FACE.

3   Int. Corridor Section. Outside Classroom.   3
Day.

AMANDA, exiting from the classroom . . . half running, as if
trying to put as much distance between her and the school as
she can.

We cut, to see GARY, inconspicuous, behind a corner,
watching AMANDA's hasty departure.

4 Ext. Street. Urban Setting. Day.   4

The desolate and downcast figure of AMANDA, trudging up
the street.

Something causes her to halt. She is looking at two GIRLS, a
year or so older than herself. Gum chewing, ear-rings
swinging, seated on a bench by the road. They are both
reading the romantic teenage magazines, now and again
nudging each other, to giggle over some article or pin-up.

AMANDA stands watching them, rooted.

We bring up, OOV, JO's words from the earlier scene.

> JO (*VO*) . . . You can see her kind everywhere . . .
> faceless, mindless girls with their heads stuck
> in those trashy magazines. They can't see
> they're being conned, they can't see anything
> except getting a boyfriend and getting married.
> It's pathetic.

*And there is a slight echo on that last word, as we hold on
AMANDA'S FACE.*

Pathetic . . .

Pathetic . . .

5 Int. Amanda's Hall. Day. Studio.   5

The quiet, empty house.

AMANDA cautiously lets herself in through the front door.

   AMANDA (*Apprehensively*) Mum?

A welcoming silence greets her.

Quickly she runs up the stairs.

A snatched impression of the room again.

All pin-ups and pop stars. And stacks and stacks of the teenage magazines littering every surface.

AMANDA enters, dumps her school bag on the bed. She catches sight of herself in the mirror, and seems unnerved slightly, or dismayed somehow, by her own reflection. She lies on the bed, arms folded behind her head, absorbed in her own thoughts.

After a moment, a familiar voice:

> PATTI Amanda? (*The disc swims into focus, to the right of Amanda's face*) Why so blue? Because of what you heard them say about you? Come on. Jealousy, that's all, because you've shown you can get yourself a fella . . .

AMANDA turns listlessly away, effectively dismissing her.

> AMANDA   (*Drearily*) I don't want to hear . . .

Once again PATTI'S DISC evaporates, to reappear, on the other side of AMANDA . . . whispering, cajoling, into her ear:

> PATTI All that nonsense about girls being mindless because all they're after is a boyfriend. A nice steady boyfriend is all anyone could want, right, Amanda? Someone to share your innermost secrets, to hold your hand through troubled times, like now? Right?

During this AMANDA starts to toss her head from side to side, as if some mute struggle is taking place . . .

PATTI That's what being a girl is all about isn't it? What all little girls are made for?

AMANDA (*Wretchedly*) No . . . no!

7 Int. Amanda's Hall. Day. Studio. 7

JUNE, is back from shopping, opening the front door, and reacting, as she hears, OOV:

AMANDA (*VO*) No . . . no . . . !

8 Int. Amanda's Bedroom. Day. Studio. 8

PATTI, whispering to AMANDA, who rocks her head back and forth, hands over ears . . .

PATTI Make it up with Gary – and if not Gary – make up to someone else! There are plenty more handsome hunks where he came from . . .

AMANDA I don't want your advice! Go away, go away . . .

JUNE (*As she enters*) Amanda? (*The disc and Patti swiftly evaporate*) What on earth's the matter? Who were you talking to?

AMANDA, however, lies quietly sobbing on the bed. JUNE crouches down next to her, still wearing her coat from the shopping trip.

JUNE What is it, tell me . . .

But AMANDA is apparently too overcome. JUNE takes her in her arms, holding her, as one would a child.

JUNE It's alright . . . come on . . . it'll be alright . . . (*Slowly Amanda's sobs subside. June gives her a handkerchief*) What did the school say?

AMANDA I . . . I'm suspended. For a week.

JUNE Oh Lord.

AMANDA I'm sorry.

JUNE (*Ruefully*) Try saying that to your father.

JUNE rises from her crouched position, and vaguely starts to tidy the room. AMANDA desolately watches her.

AMANDA Mum?

As JUNE turns to her:

AMANDA Why are things so much more difficult than they say?

JUNE (*Puzzled*) Than who says?

AMANDA Everyone, everything. The telly. Ads. Magazines . . .

JUNE Because it's easier for people to ignore the problems of life, rather than face them, I suppose.

AMANDA Why do people believe them?

JUNE Because they want to. Those old dreams are only in your head. (*Pause*) It's a song, do you know it? (*Amanda shakes her head*) Before your time, that's why.

AMANDA Were things easier then, for you?

JUNE At your age?

AMANDA Yes.

JUNE They were more straightforward. Jobs were hard to come by, but not as hard as now. There was less talk about all this nuclear business . . . less gloom and death on the news . . .

(*She glances at Amanda*) We were told we had
never had it so good, but that's not true for
youngsters now . . . if it was, you wouldn't
need to escape into these things would you?
I'm not saying it isn't good to have dreams,
Amanda, but they must lead to something.

And she looks down, at a pile of magazines in her hand.
AMANDA too looks at them. As if this thought has somehow
never occurred . . .

The front door slamming, OOV, causes them both to
react . . .

JUNE That's your dad . . . you'd better leave this
to me.

JUNE goes. AMANDA rises, to listen at the door.

9 Int. Amanda's Hall. Day. Studio.　　9

FRANK, dressed for work, about to enter the kitchen.

Hearing JUNE on the stairs he pauses.

FRANK Have you heard from the school?

JUNE (*A beat*) They sent her home. She's suspended.

Shot of FRANK'S FACE.

10 Int. Amanda's Bedroom. Day. Studio.　　10

AMANDA at the open door.

JUNE (*OOV*) For a week. I imagine they want to
make an example of her.

FRANK (*OOV*) I'll make an example of her!

JUNE (*OOV*) Frank, please . . .

Cut to:

11   Int. Hall. Day. Studio.   11

FRANK, about to march up the stairs. JUNE blocking his path.

> JUNE   Reading the riot act to her isn't going to help . . .

> FRANK   Neither is standing by and doing nothing, is it?

Cut to:

12   Int. Amanda's Bedroom. Day. Studio.   12

AMANDA's apprehensive face, by the door.

> JUNE   (*OOV*) There's nothing we can do until you've
> both calmed down . . .

> FRANK   (*OOV*) What's there to be calm about? Our
> own daughter behaves like some kind of . . .
> vandal and we're supposed to act like nothing's
> happened . . . ?

During this dialogue, AMANDA closes the door, leans against
it. The muted sounds of her parents still penetrating from
below.

She looks into the bedroom and her eye catches one stack of
her magazines, strewn over the bed once used by Katherine.

Other voices now build, obliterating those of her
parents . . .

AMANDA now looking at another pile of magazines, on the
floor by her bed.

More voices, echoing forth . . .

AMANDA covers her ears, but still the voices go on.

And the voices, whispering, husky with emotion, recede and
beckon across the room. The voices, confused and jumbled,
rise like the crest of a wave.

AMANDA presses against the door, as if threatened she'll be engulfed . . .

As the voices continue whispering at her, she swings open the door, and runs . . .

13   Int. Amanda's Hall. Day. Studio.   13

AMANDA, distraught, running down the stairs. She sprints for the front door and is just disappearing through it, when FRANK emerges from the kitchen . . .

> FRANK   Hey! I want a word with you, young lady! (*But she's gone*) Amanda!

FRANK darts after her, but too late.

He turns to see JUNE looking at him.

14   Int. Katherine's Flat. Sitting Room. Day.   14
Studio.

The BABY, mercifully quiet in a carrycot. Baby clothes and gear lying about, splashed over the sofa and chairs.

> KATHERINE   So, are you going to tell me about it?
>
> AMANDA   Nothing to tell. I didn't do it, the mural (*Looking directly at her*).
>
> KATHERINE   I didn't for a second think you did.
>
> AMANDA   (*Tartly*) Why, because I'm too mindless to act on my own?
>
> KATHERINE   Eh?
>
> AMANDA   What people think of me.

KATHERINE   You'd have to be pretty mindless if you had
             done it, wouldn't you? How was the rest of it
             anyway? Your date with thingy. (*Amanda
             gives a small shrug*) Oh?

AMANDA   Just didn't work out.

KATHERINE   Oh well, not that important is it. (*Pause*) Or is it?

AMANDA gives a small shrug.

KATHERINE   Perhaps it was just having a date that was
             important, rather than the boy himself?

AMANDA   If you want to know, he wasn't interested in
             me.

KATHERINE   What was he interested in? (*Amanda shoots her a
             look, implying it's obvious*) Ah, he made a pass
             did he?

AMANDA   Yes.

KATHERINE   Oh dear! Well it's what you wanted him to do,
             isn't it?

AMANDA   Not like that.

KATHERINE   So he bungled it, could be . . . he was as
             nervous as you.

KATHERINE only poses it as a theory, but it strikes home.

AMANDA   Who says I was nervous?

KATHERINE   People never live up to the dreams you have
             about them. Which isn't their fault, but yours
             for expecting too much.

15   Int. Amanda's Kitchen. Evening. Studio.   15

A silent, slightly preoccupied meal. Certainly from
AMANDA's viewpoint anyway.

FRANK is eating, idly reading the paper at the same time. JUNE enters from the hall and the telephone.

> JUNE That was the school . . . it seems one of the boys came clean about the mural. You can go back tomorrow.

AMANDA says nothing.

> FRANK (*With difficulty*) Amanda . . . Mandy . . . I know I was a bit hasty . . . but I was only thinking of you. Your welfare, you know that, don't you?

AMANDA, dropping her knife and fork onto the plate.

> AMANDA Sorry. I don't seem to be very hungry.

So saying, she rises and exits. MICHAEL, unperturbed, pulls AMANDA's plate towards him, and tips the food onto his own.

16   Int. Amanda's Bedroom. Evening. Studio.   16

AMANDA lying on the bed. Her radio is playing.

This is the point where we hear the theme song for the series, emanating from the radio. Re-arranged perhaps, so that it has a melancholy, poignant resonance, which both echoes and emphasises her mood.

It is important that this moment should not appear self-indulgent. It is quite simply what teenagers do at such moments, as if by hearing their dilemma or problems voiced through a pop song, they obtain, not only comfort, but a form of escape.

We hold on AMANDA'S FACE. As we do so we mix to:

Fantasy sequence. Photographic effects. AMANDA is back on
her date with GARY, and is sitting beside him on a bench.
GARY is kissing her and she is resisting him.

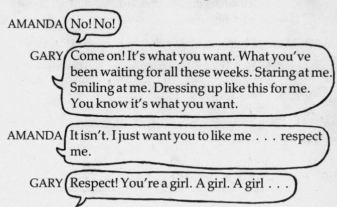

AMANDA No! No!

GARY Come on! It's what you want. What you've
been waiting for all these weeks. Staring at me.
Smiling at me. Dressing up like this for me.
You know it's what you want.

AMANDA It isn't. I just want you to like me . . . respect
me.

GARY Respect! You're a girl. A girl. A girl . . .

Cut to:

16B   Int. Amanda's Bedroom. Evening.   16B
   Studio.

Real life. AMANDA is in her bedroom, listening as the
taunting word 'GIRL' echoes on.

17   Int. Kitchen. Evening. Studio.   17

JUNE, clearing up the supper dishes. FRANK, vaguely
assisting. MICHAEL, intent on his bike speedo.

FRANK You want me to go up, talk to her?

JUNE One of us should.

MICHAEL If she wants to play silly beggars, let her.

JUNE   Oh Michael.

MICHAEL   Oh Michael what? She's a miserable cow. She loves sulking.

JUNE   I don't think she is sulking. I think she's confused and depressed and that we should help her . . .

MICHAEL   (*A grin*) She'll probably go anorexic on us next.

JUNE   We all know that you've got all the answers. It obviously hasn't struck you she might be trying to find a few of her own.

MICHAEL'S FACE, briefly, as if the truth of this does now strike. Not that he'll admit it of course.

18   Int. School Corridor. Day.   18

The section of corridor outside the classroom, as before. A huddle of GIRLS, peering through the window in the door to the classroom.

Within, we can see a MASTER confronting the BOYS – ROSS, DOMMY and MICK.

The three BOYS stand, shifting their weight uncomfortably, as a diatribe is delivered unto them. Mute to us of course, through the classroom door.

We pick out AMANDA, approaching down the corridor. She pauses by the huddle of GIRLS, peering over their shoulders.

AMANDA   What's going on?

One of the girls glances at her briefly.

GIRL   You should know. (*Amanda's face*) They're being suspended aren't they?

AMANDA   But . . . who told on them?

GIRL I'd have thought you'd know that too. (*Amanda stares at her blankly*) It was Gary, wasn't it?

So saying, she departs, leaving AMANDA looking through the window at the shifting, shifty boys.

19   Ext. School. Day.   19

JO Come on, Hilary.

HILARY It's pointless.

JO You can't blame everyone for giving up on us, if we do.

HILARY Look, I whipped up those girls into this because I believed in what we were doing, right? That we really could change something. OK, Amanda may not have done it herself, but she never really cared about it, none of them did. From now on I intend looking after number one and they can look after themselves. We were stupid and naive to think we could change things by one gesture anyway. I'm going to learn by that, if you're not.

HILARY exits. Hold on JO and POLLY submitting to the logic of her words.

20   Int. Classroom. Day. Studio.   20

Desks are being pushed back, a circle of chairs being arranged. MISS SULLIVAN at the centre of it all, a pile of books in hand, organising and supervising.

MISS
SULLIVAN Today, a contemporary poet. Stevie Smith. (*Chairs continue to be scraped as places are taken*) Come on, settle down. Someone get the door please. (*Pause*) We'll start by choosing a poem,

> reading and analysing it. That way we'll begin
> to understand something of her imagery and
> themes . . . then we'll take it from there.

She starts to leaf through the book of poems.

The class are now all seated, similarly engaged.

MISS
SULLIVAN Page forty-four, I think. 'Not Waving but
Drowning.' Amanda? Perhaps you'd like to
read it for us.

AMANDA'S FACE, colouring slightly in apprehension.

GARY steals a look at her.

MISS SULLIVAN addresses the rest of the group.

MISS
SULLIVAN While I think of it, we've got the careers officer
coming next month. Ask in the general office
for an appointment. You should think
seriously about seeing him. Contrary to
popular opinion, there is life after school you
know. (*A ripple from the class at this*) Right,
Amanda, when you're ready.

*AMANDA starts to read. She does it extremely well, she doesn't
stumble or falter, and she clearly understands, and is moved by what
she reads.*

AMANDA 'Nobody heard him the dead man,
But still he lay moaning;
I was much further out than you thought
And not waving, but drowning.
(*A shot of the class watching, struck as much by her
delivery as the words themselves*)

> Poor chap, he always loved larking
> And now he's dead
> It must have been too cold for him,
> > his heart gave way,
>
> They said.
> (*A shot of Polly now, watching her friend*)
> Oh, no no no, it was too cold always
> (Still the dead one lay moaning)
> I was much too far out all my life
> And not waving . . . but drowning.'

A small silence. MISS SULLIVAN glances around the class.

MISS
SULLIVAN   Good. Fine. Now then, the repeated refrain, 'not waving, but drowning'. Any ideas on it's meaning. Amanda?

AMANDA   People thought . . . he was waving at them, but he was really drowning.

MISS
SULLIVAN   And?

AMANDA looks down at the poem a moment.

AMANDA   Well later . . . where it says . . . 'I was much too far out all my life, not waving but drowning . . . ' She means . . . that people always got him wrong. All his life.

POLLY'S FACE here, once more, watching her friend.

MISS
SULLIVAN   And what was he drowning in – in the context of this poem. Gary?

GARY   Erm . . . life?

MISS
SULLIVAN   Explain.

GARY   Perhaps he couldn't cope. Couldn't handle it.
And no-one ever knew.

MISS
SULLIVAN   Couldn't cope with what aspects of life do you
suppose?

POLLY   That's for the reader to decide, surely? It could
be anything.

MISS
SULLIVAN   Like what?

POLLY   (*After a moment*) Despair. That he was
despairing somehow.

MISS
SULLIVAN   Of life, or himself?

POLLY   Well, both.

MISS
SULLIVAN   Do you go along with that Amanda?

AMANDA   . . . It says 'It must have been too cold for
him . . . '

MISS
SULLIVAN   So?

AMANDA   Like he was very alone . . . because . . . if you
feel alone . . . feel lonely . . . you despair
more easily. And drowning . . . it's like
being alone as well. It's the same kind of
feeling.

Cut to:

21   Int. Bike Shed. School. Day.   21

A jumble of pupils and bikes. An end-of-the-day
atmosphere.

AMANDA is crouched by her bicycle pumping a tyre. She glances up to see GARY standing over her. His own bike by his side.

> GARY (*Awkwardly*) Look . . . it wasn't my idea . . . the mural and everything . . . I was against it from the start.

> AMANDA I know.

He stares at her a moment.

> GARY Why didn't you say something then? Why let them think it was you?

> AMANDA (*A shrug*) It didn't seem to matter.

> GARY (*As she looks at him*) It mattered to me.

POLLY appears, slightly breathless.

> POLLY Oh Mandy, there you are. Erm . . . is it OK if I call round tonight? Only I wanted to talk to you . . .

> AMANDA (*Without rancour, simply like a statement of fact*) With me, or Michael?

POLLY studies her a moment.

> POLLY You. Actually.

She goes.

> GARY (*Picking up where he left off*) It hasn't exactly made me very popular you know.

> AMANDA Is that why you did it?

> GARY No it isn't.

He clambers onto his bike. His tone throwaway, but it hits the mark none-the-less.

> GARY Though I wonder now why I bothered.

He cycles off.

AMANDA'S FACE, that ruefulness there once more. Is she always going to handle things this badly?

Cut to:

22   Int. Amanda's Garage. Day. Studio.   22

MICHAEL, underneath his bike, attaching the speedo or whatever. POLLY is watching.

We pick them up in mid-conversation.

> POLLY   She's avoiding me, its obvious. Why else would she say she was baby-sitting?

> MICHAEL   You can catch up with her at school can't you?

> POLLY   Not to speak to.

> MICHAEL   I hope you're not going in for all this stupid malarky as well. (*Polly's face*) She's got everyone running round in circles, hasn't she? Why all the big deal?

> POLLY   She happens to be my best friend. (*Pause*) Or she was. (*As he glances at her*) You and I put pay to that, didn't we?

> MICHAEL   Why for Pete's sake?

> POLLY   You're not that dense.

His face – blank.

> POLLY   (*As if stating the obvious*) Because when I used to call round it was to see her, wasn't it? Before you came on the scene.

> MICHAEL   We always asked her to tag along didn't we? Made a point of it.

> POLLY   (*A beat*) Too much of a point perhaps.

162

MICHAEL   Is this some roundabout way of saying you
            want to pack it in or something?

POLLY   Of course not. (*She gets off the side to pace
            about, as if working out something out loud*)
            Somehow our . . . getting together has been at
            her expense. Or at least at the expense of our
            friendship. It's . . . complicated things.
            Mandy and me . . . we did everything
            together. And suddenly she has to watch all
            that . . . be given to someone else. And worse
            still, her own brother.

MICHAEL   Thanks very much.

POLLY   She's jealous, don't you see?

MICHAEL   If she's jealous, it's of Katherine. Getting
            married. A place of her own. A kid of her own.
            It's all she's ever dreamed of. Always has been.
            (*Polly's face*) What all girls dream of, right?

23   Int. Katherine's Kitchen. Day. Studio.   23

KATHERINE and TERRY getting ready to go out.

AMANDA is going to baby-sit.

KATHERINE   I'll pop this in the fridge for later, alright?
            Don't give it to her unless she starts, though,
            will you? Are you sure you can manage?

TERRY   Come on, Kath. One night out and it turns
            into a Duke of Edinburgh Award Scheme . . .

AMANDA   Go on!

TERRY   Kath, come on!

AMANDA   Have a nice time.

KATHERINE We won't be late.

TERRY and KATHERINE leave.

24   Int. Katherine's Living Room. Day.   24

AMANDA looks about, at the baby gear and lunch plates still on the table.

The BABY clearly isn't settled.

Then she switches on the television, the BABY squirming on her lap. The news is on, and we pick up the newsreader, reading an item . . .

> NEWS-
> READER Now, unemployment. A recent report shows that once again the school leaver is the hardest hit.

AMANDA rises abruptly to switch off the television. She turns to look at the BABY, innocently burbling at her.

Once again, AMANDA'S FACE as the BABY gurgles and twists in her arms.

25   Int. Amanda's Kitchen. Night. Studio.   25

JUNE is in the kitchen making a hot drink.

AMANDA has let herself in with her door key. She enters the kitchen and sits down.

> JUNE How did it go?

> AMANDA . . . I thought babies were supposed to sleep all the time?

> JUNE (*Smile*) Whatever gave you that idea? Er . . . your father's in the garage. Take this to him will you?

FRANK is busy at the work bench, putting the final touches to a powered model aeroplane.

Now that we can see the garage properly we should see other examples of Frank's handiwork. Other model aeroplanes in various states of disrepair. A few framed photographs even, on the walls, showing Frank, proudly holding one of his miniature aircraft . . .

AMANDA enters, and sets down the hot drink.

> FRANK   Cheers, love. (*Glancing at her*) Baby-sitting go OK?

> AMANDA   Fine.

FRANK is obviously building to speak, but hasn't properly worked out just what it is he wants to say.

> FRANK   Your er . . . mother said you were a bit down at the moment? (*Amanda gives a small shrug*) About this boy or . . . ?

> AMANDA   Not really.

> FRANK   Everything's cleared up at school though?

> AMANDA   Oh yes.

A small silence. AMANDA touches the aeroplane.

> AMANDA   Looks OK.

> FRANK   All but a lick of paint and it's done. I'll test fly her at the weekend. (*He picks up the model, examining it*). I always had a dream you know, that one day I'd fly. Not these little beggars. A full sized light weight. A Tiger Moth or . . . Got half way to getting my pilot's licence too.

> AMANDA   (*Curiously*) What stopped you?

FRANK   Oh, money. Raising a family. Little things like that. (*Pause*) Dreams come pretty expensive, one way and another.

AMANDA   Yes.

He glances at her.

FRANK   What do you dream about?

AMANDA   Me?

FRANK   Boys, travel, what?

AMANDA gives a slightly awkward shrug.

FRANK   Do you mind me asking?

AMANDA   You know.

FRANK   No, I don't. I was standing here tonight. Your mother let slip you were down. And I suddenly realised I didn't know. Didn't know my own kids. Not what went on in their heads at any rate.

AMANDA   I'm not sure I know what's going on in my head myself. (*Then*) Sometimes I . . .

She pauses.

FRANK   Yes?

AMANDA   I look at Katherine. At the baby. And I think . . . is this what it's all about? There must be something more, surely?

FRANK   There is, if you reach out and grab it. (*A pause*) What I'm really doing, when I sound off at you the way I do. Lose my bottle. It's because of the dreams I've got for you. Getting on in the world. Making something of yourself. And when I see all that threatened . . . I lash out.

(*Amanda's face. It's very quiet suddenly, just his voice, talking*) You do that with children. It's a way of handling it.

AMANDA Handling what?

FRANK Despair.

AMANDA looks at him sharply.

AMANDA You feel that too?

FRANK We all feel it, from time to time. Oh yes, me too. We just try and distract ourselves as best we can. Why else would a grown man spend so much time playing with toys?

AMANDA'S FACE. He smiles at her slowly. Almost ruefully, she smiles back. As if there is some kind of new understanding there.

27 Int. Amanda's Bedroom. Night. Studio. 27

AMANDA, lying in bed, arms folded thinking . . .

She glances sideways, to the magazines, strewn across Katherine's bed.

Once again, voices quietly issue from them . . .

But not just the voices of the magazine characters. Mixed in with them, and eventually overriding them, are other voices. Snatches of what has been said of her, and to her, over the last day or so.

JO (*VO*) Mindless faceless girls, they can't see they're being conned . . .

AMANDA (*VO*) I was much too far out all my life, not just waving but . . .

KATHERINE (*VO*) People never live up to the dreams you have of them, which isn't their fault, but yours, for expecting too much . . .

FRANK *(VO)* Achieve something; get on in the world . . .

AMANDA *(VO)* I was much too far out all my life . . .

FRANK *(VO)* Just to reach out and grab it . . .

The voices blend and bleed together.

We move steadily on AMANDA'S FACE. Freeze frame.

PATTI'S VOICE OVER now, all bright and brisk optimism.

PATTI *(VO)* Will Amanda ever get over her blues?

Are *all* her dreams really in her head?

. . . To be concluded . . . next week.

End of Episode Five

A closer look at . . .

Marriage

Marriage is still a very popular institution. In Western culture it is usually linked to sentimental and romantic images: white lace and satin, pink hearts, love and devotion that will continue for eternity. Have you noticed that in many books and magazines this is where the story ends: the bride and groom get married and live happily ever after. They have succeeded, made it, full stop. Complications, problems, and disappointments are a thing of the past. The future is rosy and happy.

We like to think that in life this is also true. But the facts of our everyday life seem to tell us otherwise. It is interesting to look at the long-standing relationships of the people you know – maybe parents, grandparents, or neighbours. Are they what you would call happy? What kind of relationship would you like to have when you are fifty years old? People often question why the divorce rate appears to be rising so fast. It is also interesting to discuss why so many people do stay together for such a long time. Is it love for one person, the security of being part of a couple, or maybe the practicalities of the situation? Is it natural to think you can live with one person for thirty or forty years? Why *do* people get married?

Most people get married in their twenties and some even earlier. This means that they have most of their lives ahead of them – maybe fifty years or more. It is a nonsense to believe that everything has been achieved, every problem solved. Look at the people around you – your parents and friends. How are they living their lives?

In *S.W.A.L.K.* Amanda still thinks that the white dress and wedding day are what matter. Katherine is beginning to realise that this is not the case. Their parents, June and Frank, are also going through a painful period of realisation –

169

their hopes and expectations are constantly dashed. Try and imagine your parents' past history, their childhood and youth. Ask them to tell you about when they were young. What were they like at school? How did they spend their time when teenagers? Their lives, like yours, have been constantly changing and developing. They have not always been as you see them now. Having children, getting to know different people, and living with each other, will have changed them. When they were young, what hopes did they have for their future? Are they disappointed with how things have actually turned out?

Life isn't lived in a romantic haze, it is full of practical day-to-day realities: money, jobs, bringing up children, sharing responsibilities. Which question would you ask when thinking of marriage or a long-term partnership: 'Do I love this person?' or 'Do I want to live with this person daily, with everything that involves, for years?' 'Will we get the support we need from society around us?' Society seems to expect us to couple up – and functioning socially as a couple is often easier than as a single person. There is also, as we can see from *S.W.A.L.K.* a great deal of encouragement from the world of magazines, television, and pop music to look at the world in an unreal, romantic way rather than in a practical, realistic one. How can we ensure that we love real people in a real way?

EPISODE SIX

'Shaping Up'

Synopsis

The recriminations over the mural are resolved, but Amanda's personal dilemma is not. Her growing impatience with Patti turns to intolerance as she comes to understand where her romantic notions end – and the price that must be paid for them.

Katherine reluctantly consents to her baby being christened. However, it is a capitulation, not just to the demands of society, but to the knowledge that her own youth has ended.

Amanda for her part sees the careers officer at school. Instead of providing solutions, he causes her to question herself. She finally realises that only she can provide the answers. In this sense too, her youth has ended. This fact is confirmed when she destroys all her romantic teenage magazines and Patti is relegated to the dustbin where she belongs.

But for all that it is not a happy ending for our final image is of Katherine's baby daughter, obliviously kicking in her pram. Patti's face appears beside her, malignant and cajoling, whispering her promises of a rosy, golden future of men and matrimony.

And the story of indoctrination continues . . .

1   Int. Katherine's Kitchen. Day.   1

The magazines, once more in an untidy, unruly pile.

They are lying on the floor, scattered in front of the washing machine, which spins noisily in the background.

1A   Standard Int. Magazine Montage.   1A

The voices as usual, emanating from them. Whispering and tearful, trembling with tenderness. The frozen, ballooned images fill the screen . . . girls and boys in poses of confrontation and adoration, drifting and merging with the sounds which accompany them.

The voices fuse and overlap . . . Patti's Problem Page drifts into shot.

As the voices rise and swell, abrupt cut to silence:

1B   Sub-Titles   1B

Bring up the episode title:

Episode Six, 'Shaping Up'.

Cut to:

1C   Int. Katherine's Flat. Day.   1C

A wider shot, we now see that the magazines are strewn in front of the washing machine for mopping up purposes.

The washing machine is clearly leaking.

KATHERINE is crouched beside it, dumping down more magazines and newspapers, to soak up the dampness.

OOV, we hear the sound of a radio and a Disc Jockey.

> DJ   (*VO*) and now, for all those lovely ladies doing such a terrific job on the domestic front . . . a little ditty especially for you.

The song *Love and Marriage* now starts. It serves only to aggravate KATHERINE's mood. She rises, rubbing her hands on her jeans and moves to the kitchen table.

The BABY is in a carrycot on a stand, in a corner. Baby bottles, piles of nappies, babygrows and baby books, clutter the kitchen.

She looks at them, quite flatly, dejectedly.

OOV, we hear the sound of the door bell. KATHERINE barely seems to register it at first, but when it rings again, drearily exits, to answer it.

1D   Int. Katherine's Sitting Room. Hall. Day. 1D

KATHERINE, opening the front door.

JUNE is there, in a raincoat, shopping bags in her arms.

> JUNE   I was on my way to the shops. Thought I'd cadge a cup of coffee.

KATHERINE says nothing, but simply leads the way into the flat.

JUNE'S FACE, slightly perplexed, not to say concerned.

2   Int. Miss Sullivan's Office. Day.   2

MISS SULLIVAN, entering.

With her is THOMAS DWIGHT, the CAREERS OFFICER. He's a man in his late forties. He's got a tiredness about him, as if he's seen everything, and life rarely, if ever, surprises him. Despite his efforts, he no longer understands the young people he meets.

> MISS
> SULLIVAN   I'm putting you in my office, it's less public than the common room.

> DWIGHT   There've been times when I've had to make do with a desk in a corridor.

He starts to unload his briefcase as they continue talking.

DWIGHT   What kind of turn-out can I expect?

MISS
SULLIVAN   I have had a word with the younger ones . . .
the Fourth Years . . . see if they're interested
as well.

DWIGHT   Righteo.

But his tone implies something like indifference.

MISS
SULLIVAN   (*A small smile*) Such enthusiasm.

DWIGHT   It's not my enthusiasm which is in question
is it?

MISS SULLIVAN'S FACE, digesting this.

3   Int. Katherine's Living Room. Day.   3

The empty coffee cups are on the table.

JUNE is just re-entering from the kitchen.

JUNE   At least you've the baby settled into a routine.
She's flat out.

KATHERINE   (*A flat note there*) Oh yes, no-one can say we're
not in a routine.

JUNE glances at her, uncertain how to take this.

She belts her raincoat and drains her coffee.

JUNE   Is there anything I can get you from the shops?

KATHERINE simply shakes her head.

JUNE picks up her shopping bags. She seems to be building
up to saying something. But her daughter's frame of mind is
clearly an inhibition. Nevertheless, she decides to plunge in.

JUNE   Your father and I were talking last night.
(*Katherine glances at her, slightly suspiciously*)
We were wondering what you planned on
doing about a christening?

KATHERINE *simply stares at her.*

JUNE   (*Slightly defensive*) Well it's a way of welcoming
a new arrival in a family, isn't it?

KATHERINE   Maybe some of us don't feel like welcoming
her. (*Now it's JUNE's turn to stare at her*) Come
on, Mum, you didn't, did you, when I told you
she was on the way? Neither of you did. It'll be
the end of everything, you said. 'The end of
life as you know it!' Well I should have
listened. You were right.

It's her tone, as much as her words, that dismay JUNE.

JUNE   We all say things . . .

KATHERINE   In the heat of the moment, I know. (*Then*)
Oh, let's just forget it. I'm just not in the mood,
OK?

JUNE   (*Slightly stiff*) Very well. If you feel that way.

KATHERINE   Yes, I feel that way, mother! Oh I know you
think I've made my bed, so now I must lie in it!
But you had a hand in it too, oh yes. All those
red faces whenever I asked about sex. All that
changing the subject and leaving the room.
You just left me to find out about it for myself.
Which is exactly what I did, isn't it?

JUNE   That simply isn't fair . . .

KATHERINE   (*Overriding her*) Fair! My God – tell that to the
baby – it's too late to waste your breath on me.

JUNE regards her daughter steadily, almost coldly, but that
too, is just her own device to cover her emotions.

175

JUNE I have never, ever, tried to keep you in the dark.
About sex or anything else. You think because
I'm your mother, I've got all the answers. Well I
haven't. Anymore than you have.

And she goes.

KATHERINE sits a moment, without moving. If she regrets
the conversation with her mother, she is too tired, too
exhausted, to even register it.

After a second, she moves to put the coffee cups on the tray.
Then she moves towards the kitchen.

4   Int. Katherine's Kitchen. Day.   4

KATHERINE, entering with the coffee cups.

A small sound from the BABY alerts her, and she crosses to it.
As she does, she freezes.

The BABY is awake, and is lying next to a small bottle.
KATHERINE with a gasp, snatches it out of the carrycot.

We should get a glimpse of it. It's clearly a pill bottle.

Now empty.

KATHERINE Dear God! Mum! Mother . . . ! (*She runs out,*
towards *the front door, and flings it open*)
Mother . . . !

But JUNE is long since gone. Panting, slightly, her breath
coming in short gasps, like sobs, KATHERINE plucks up a
shawl, and roughly wraps it around the BABY, and then
literally runs, still panting and sobbing, out of the flat.

5   Ext. Streets (Urban). Day.   5

KATHERINE, hurtling down a street, the BABY in her arms.

By-standers scattering, as she careers through them.

6   Int. School Corridor. Day.   6

Another sprinting figure, this time AMANDA. Dashing down
the corridor . . . To crash into a BOY approaching in the
opposite direction.

AMANDA Sorry.

And she's off, leaving him reeling.

7   Int. Girls Toilet. Day.   7

POLLY, washing her hands.

AMANDA reels in.

AMANDA Did I miss registration?

POLLY I'll say. What kept you?

AMANDA Ruddy bus. What else?

*She dumps down her school bag and moves to enter a toilet. POLLY
continues washing her hands.*

POLLY The er . . . careers officer's in today. You fancy
giving him a whirl?

AMANDA (*OOV*) Is there any point?

POLLY One way of finding out isn't there?

AMANDA now emerges from the toilet.

AMANDA OK. Where is he?

POLLY Miss Sullivan's room. One problem though.

AMANDA pauses, waiting.

POLLY (*Cont*) Means we miss domestic science.

And she says it as if this is something like a tragedy.

AMANDA pulls a face, as if matching her tone, and then they both giggle, and scurry out. Something of their former friendship regained.

8   Int. Miss Sullivan's Office. Day.   8

DWIGHT, pinning up posters on careers on a pinboard, advertising various job prospects and qualifications.

MISS SULLIVAN, aiding him, but distractedly, her attention caught momentarily, now and again, by a leaflet or a poster.

MISS
SULLIVAN   There used to be a list . . . 'Careers for Girls' remember? Everything from C for Chamber maids to K for Kennel maids.

DWIGHT   There's some would prefer we went back to it.

MISS
SULLIVAN   Back to what?

DWIGHT   The old segregation system. Nice gentle undemanding jobs for the girls and tough professional ones for the boys.

MISS
SULLIVAN   (*Curiously*) Like who?

DWIGHT   The girls themselves. (*She looks at him in surprise*) Oh you can make a law to stop differentiating between the sexes . . . you can tell them until you're blue in the face that they're equal to the boys . . . but it's what they tell themselves which really counts.

MISS SULLIVAN	(*After a moment*) And where do we fit into all this? Or don't we?
DWIGHT	The theory is, we can throw a spanner in the works. Throw them a challenge and hope they rise to it.
MISS SULLIVAN	And if they don't?
DWIGHT	They'll carry on being the good obedient girls they've been brought up to be, won't they? They'll go obediently into some typing pool, walk obediently up the aisle, and end up, obediently pushing a pram about.
MISS SULLIVAN	(*A beat. She's curious about his defeatist, rather laconic tone, and a little annoyed by it*) Isn't it *your* job to make them face up to these things?
DWIGHT	I'm not a miracle worker. I can't make the blind see. (*Then, carelessly, like an afterthought*) Hang around if you like. Find out for yourself.

MISS SULLIVAN'S FACE. Once again, accepting a challenge.

9   Ext. Hospital. Casualty. Day.   9

KATHERINE, running into the casualty and accident outpatients. The BABY clutched in her arms.

10   Int. Section Corridor. Ext. Miss Sullivan's   10
Office. Day.

Just a small section of corridor, like a waiting area, we see the notice on the door again . . . 'Careers Officer.'

179

POLLY and AMANDA, amongst one or two others, seated, waiting.

In the background a GIRL rises to enter the careers office.

POLLY is building up to speak, as if she wants to confide in AMANDA, but has somehow lost the knack.

POLLY (*A casual note*) I was round at your place last night.

AMANDA Oh? How are things?

As Polly glances at her.

AMANDA With Michael.

POLLY (*Bluntly*) Round in bleeding circles, since you ask. (*Now it's Amanda's turn to glance at her*) He doesn't take anything seriously, does he? Ever. He seems to make a joke out of everything.

AMANDA (*Wryly*) You've spotted that have you?

POLLY Whenever I try to talk, you know, about anything, anything at all, he starts wise-cracking all over the place. Like he's . . . frightened to be serious or something.

AMANDA (*Curiously*) I thought it was serious, between you and him.

POLLY Some chance. The thing is . . . I'm glad it isn't, in a way. It would be stupid. I know that. But if you're not involved . . . if there isn't anything there, where's it all supposed to be going? Where's the point in it?

AMANDA Have you told him all this?

POLLY He'd just laugh it off, wouldn't he? And it's not just me he won't take seriously. That's half the trouble. It's girls in general.

On the line, cut to:

11   Int. Careers Office. Day.   11

DWIGHT, on one side of the desk, the GIRL on the other. MISS SULLIVAN seated nearby.

We should be able to see, from her manner, and his, that the interview is going rather awkwardly. Clearly it's hard work, on both sides.

DWIGHT Let's put your school work to one side for a moment. How about hobbies? A career can just as easily spring out of a leisure pursuit as an academic one.

The GIRL regards him listlessly for a moment.

GIRL Don't really have any.

DWIGHT You must do something with your spare time?

GIRL (*After a moment of lip biting*) Listen to music?

DWIGHT Pop music?

GIRL (*A limp attempt at humour*) What other sort is there? And I watch TV of course.

View of DWIGHT'S FACE.

GIRL And I read a bit.

DWIGHT cheers up.

DWIGHT Good. Excellent. What kind of reading?

GIRL You know. *Oh Boy, Jackie, Mates*. Usual kind of thing.

DWIGHT'S FACE again.

> DWIGHT   (*Another tack*) How about your parents? Have
> you discussed your future with them at all?

> GIRL   Sometimes.

> DWIGHT   And?

> GIRL   And what?

It's like drawing blood from a stone.

> DWIGHT   What advice have they given you?

> GIRL   None. Well, I'll probably get married won't I?

*DWIGHT, casting a kind of 'I told you so' expression to MISS
SULLIVAN.*

> GIRL   Mind you, there is one thing I'd quite like to do.

> DWIGHT   Oh?

> GIRL   Probably not on though.

> DWIGHT   (*Eagerly*) We'll know that when you tell us
> what it is.

The GIRL seems bashful suddenly.

> MISS
> SULLIVAN   Come on, Sarah.

> DWIGHT   Spit it out, love, that's what we're here for.

> GIRL   What I'd really like to do, is be a lion-tamer.

Shot of DWIGHT'S EXPRESSION.

---

12 Int. Hospital Casualty Cubicle. Day.   12

Just a curtained cubicle, minimal size. Sounds of the hospital
life, OOV.

A white-coated DOCTOR is examining the BABY. A NURSE is stooped over KATHERINE, nearby. KATHERINE is still very distraught.

> NURSE   (*A pen and clipboard to the ready*) Try and calm yourself, love, please. What kind of pills were they?

> KATHERINE   (*Her eyes on the baby*) Tranquillisers.

> NURSE   (*Making a note*) Were they prescribed by a doctor?

> KATHERINE   (*Nodding*) I was only out of the room a few minutes and . . .

> NURSE   . . . What sort of tranquillisers?

KATHERINE makes no reply. She's still watching the BABY, her attention focussed entirely on it.

> NURSE   What type of tranquillisers, try and think, please.

> KATHERINE   Valium.

> NURSE   How many were left? Approximately.

> KATHERINE   I don't remember . . . that's just the point . . . I don't remember!

> NURSE   And who were they prescribed for?

KATHERINE'S FACE now, as if the question surprises her.

> KATHERINE   Me of course.

13   Int. Careers Office. Day.   13

POLLY is now facing DWIGHT over the table.

MISS SULLIVAN sitting in, as before.

> DWIGHT   Well, where do your interests lie?

POLLY ponders this a moment.

> POLLY School-wise?

> DWIGHT In general.

> POLLY Languages I suppose. It's what I'm best at.
> (*Then cautiously*) I thought perhaps . . .
> university?

> DWIGHT Do you think you're up to it?

POLLY stares at him a moment, frowning.

> POLLY Why d'you say that? (*His face*) As if . . . well . . .
> without giving me a chance.

MISS SULLIVAN smiles slightly, as if a small point has been scored for her side.

> DWIGHT I'm simply asking you a question others will
> ask you.

> POLLY How does anyone know I'm not up to it?

MISS SULLIVAN'S SMILE broadens. She's starting to enjoy herself.

14 Int. Hospital Casualty Cubicle. Day. 14

KATHERINE, now alone, agitatedly waiting.

The NURSE enters.

> NURSE We've cleared her stomach out. There's
> nothing. Apart from some discomfort, there's
> nothing wrong at all. There's really no way
> there could be. She's far too young to put
> anything in her mouth herself. (*Katherine's
> face*) Perhaps you finished the pills. They can
> make one rather forgetful.

> KATHERINE I . . . just saw the empty bottle and . . . (*She
> starts to sob*) Oh God . . . I'm such a fool . . .
> such a bloody fool!

It's said half in relief, but also out of an acute despair. The NURSE tries to comfort her.

KATHERINE   She is alright? You're sure?

NURSE   (*A smile*) I think you can say there's life in her yet.

We hear ths sound of the BABY screaming and crying. It's a sound which usually makes KATHERINE wince, but today, it's music to her ears.

15   Int. Careers Office. Day.   15

AMANDA is now rather nervously facing DWIGHT.

AMANDA   Am I supposed to've filled up a form or something?

DWIGHT   I don't think we have to be that formal just yet. (*Then*) So, do you plan on staying at school to take A levels or . . . ?

AMANDA   Hadn't really thought about it.

DWIGHT   What do you see yourself doing, in five years say? Ideally. If you had the choice?

PATTI'S DISC appears beside Amanda.

PATTI   (*A whisper*) Amanda . . . listen to me, Amanda . . . not to him.

DWIGHT   Something scientific? Artistic perhaps?

AMANDA   Er . . . Artistic I suppose.

DWIGHT   How about maths, how are you on that? (*Amanda pulls a face*) What's sixteen away from sixty?

PATTI He's just trying to trap you . . . to make you look stupid. Don't answer him!

AMANDA Erm . . . (*A painful pause*) Forty-four?

DWIGHT Correct, which is precisely the amount of working years you've got ahead of you, assuming you leave school at sixteen and retire at sixty. (*Amanda's face*) Unless of course you decide to make that forty years, and stay on at school or college and get some extra qualifications.

PATTI Qualifications! Qualifications! If there are all these wonderful jobs around, how come he ends up a boring old careers officer, eh?

AMANDA But, I mean . . . women don't usually work that long, do they?

PATTI Good one, Mandy! Let's see him try and wriggle out of that.

MISS
SULLIVAN They could, if they wanted to. Even with bringing up a family.

AMANDA Only the really bright ones.

DWIGHT The girl in before you accused me of dismissing her without giving her a chance. Now you're dismissing yourself. Why? (*Amanda says nothing*)

PATTI gives a wide, gaping yawn.

PATTI He, ho . . .

DWIGHT The fact is anyone can do anything if they want to. Because it all depends on if you really want to get yourself a career of some kind . . . or just go through the motions.

AMANDA I wouldn't have come at all if that was it, would I?

DWIGHT The point is I can only tell you what's involved. The rest you have to do for yourself.

She says nothing. We should sense he's anxious to reach her suddenly. He didn't mean to lecture, merely to be reasonably honest with her.

DWIGHT It seems unwelcoming out there. And hostile, right? And it is, no point in pretending otherwise. When it actually comes to facing it, you can do one of two things. Lose yourself in marriage and babies, or you can decide to have a go and have a family later.

AMANDA'S FACE, listening.

AMANDA Have a go at what?

DWIGHT Have a go at changing it. God knows there's plenty about it could do with changing.

PATTI What does he think you are? A miracle worker?

AMANDA How can I change anything? I'm just me. One person.

MISS
SULLIVAN If you're bright enough to ask that, you should be able to work out the reply.

AMANDA looks at MISS SULLIVAN, and then at DWIGHT. They simply wait.

PATTI (Don't fall for it, Amanda! Just get up and walk out – we've wasted enough time on these creeps already . . . come on! Just stand up and walk out!)

AMANDA doesn't move.

AMANDA (*Ignoring Patti. She pauses, frowning in concentration*) If you change yourself . . . or how you feel about yourself, other people will change how they feel about you. I mean . . . you may not change the world, but you can change . . . well, the way you fit into it.

AMANDA regards them both, not as if seeking approval, but to see if she has made her point comprehensible.

From their faces, it is evident that she has.

16   Int. Katherine's Flat. Kitchen. Day.   16

The BABY, kicking on a changing mat. KATHERINE attending to a nappy.

She looks strained by the events of the day, but not entirely defeated by them. AMANDA sits watching her.

AMANDA How come you've been taking tranquillisers anyway?

KATHERINE I just get jumpy sometimes. It's being on my own so much. Anything can get out of proportion if you think about it enough.

AMANDA Mum'd have a fit if she knew you took stuff like that.

KATHERINE Is she going to know? You know, until I got that shock with her today, I don't think I ever really loved her. Not properly. I cared for her, looked after her, but I always . . .

resented her. I kept remembering what it was like before. The old single life. Even that crummy job didn't seem so bad when I came to look back on it. (*She glances at Amanda. Then*) They did an experiment once, on people to make them see what having a child was like. They tied an egg onto a piece of string and then tied it onto a person's wrist. Twenty four hours a day for days. (*Amanda giggles at this*) I'm not kidding. They had to sleep with it, go to work with it, go to the loo with it, the lot. The idea was to make people see what it felt like, being tied to someone else every second of every day. Which is what I resented most of all I think.

She looks at the BABY, as if working something through her mind.

AMANDA   I know what you mean.

17   Int. Amanda's Bedroom. Day.   17

AMANDA, at a table in her room.

She has a pile of school books in front of her – homework we may safely conclude. She is sitting, as the scene opens, pen in hand, thinking. Then she seems to shrug her thoughts off, and concentrate on her school work.

As she does so, PATTI'S DISC swims into shot, right of frame. She smiles indulgently at AMANDA's bowed and studied head.

PATTI   Oh Amanda? (*Amanda winces, and shifts her position so that her back is turned to Patti*) Not too busy to talk to your old mate are you?

18 Int. Kitchen. Amanda's House. Day. 18

FRANK, cleaning his shoes. JUNE, brushing her hair. They
are getting ready to go to KATHERINE's. MICHAEL and POLLY
sit at the table, cups of tea before them.

JUNE She wants to talk to us about the christening.

MICHAEL Christening! Do me a favour. No one bothers
about christening kids these days, do they?

FRANK That makes it all A.OK does it?

MICHAEL What's the point in it – it's not as if Kath and
Terry are even religious.

JUNE It's just a custom, isn't it?

MICHAEL Sounds pretty hypocritical to me.

FRANK Have you ever *been* to a christening, as a matter
of interest?

MICHAEL No.

FRANK Then it seems pretty hypocritical to give an
opinion on something you know nothing
about.

MICHAEL and POLLY, exchanging a long suffering look.

19 Int. Amanda's Bedroom. Day. 19

AMANDA, steadfastly concentrating on her books.

PATTI, in her disc, simpering in her ear.

PATTI Work's all very well, but there's a time and
place, right? And we've got more important
things to talk about.

A flicker of irritation as AMANDA continues writing.

PATTI Like a certain husky fella by the name of
       Gary . . . ?

*And once again, AMANDA shifts her position, but PATTI is not
easily deterred. The disc shifts and the simpering continues.*

PATTI You know if you don't do something soon,
       you'll miss the boat altogether, Amanda.
       Can't have that, can we? No boyfriend at your
       age – people'll start to think there's something
       wrong with you.

*AMANDA'S FACE again, a look of calculated forebearance there.
JUNE, OOV, mercifully intercedes.*

       JUNE (*OOV*) We're off, Amanda – are you ready?

*AMANDA starts to close her school books, and put the cap on her
pen.*

PATTI No hurry . . . besides, I haven't finished with
       you yet. Not by a long way.

AMANDA slams the last book closed and rises. And she stomps off.

PATTI Lovely! Charming! Without me you're nothing,
       you hear that? A big flat zero! Say goodbye to
       me and you'll say goodbye to romance and
       boys and fun! You hear me! You'll be on your
       own!

On her indignant face, cut to:

20   Int. Katherine's Kitchen. Evening.   20

The room is relatively clean and tidy. The table is being laid
by KATHERINE. TERRY is pacing, the BABY in his arms. A
nappy over one shoulder, to catch spillage.

TERRY And who's going to fork out for it? It's just a farce. We didn't even get married in a church, did we?

KATHERINE It's got nothing to do with that.

TERRY Why bother then?

KATHERINE The way things are. It'll be on her school forms, on her record. . .

TERRY Who gives a damn about all that stuff?

KATHERINE (*Pointing, almost angrily at the world beyond the window*) They do. And if we didn't care about what they think we'd never have got married at all, would we? (*His face*) We couldn't beat the system, so we joined it. She may as well too! (*She exits. We hold on* TERRY, *the* BABY *in his arms*)

21 Int. Amanda's Kitchen. Evening. 21

POLLY, slightly preoccupied at the table. MICHAEL is in the kitchen area.

MICHAEL You want another coffee or something? (*She shakes her head*) Beer? There's half a can in the fridge.

POLLY No thanks.

MICHAEL takes the beer for himself. He lounges against the fridge, watching her.

MICHAEL (*Casualness itself*) How about coming up to my room. We could listen to some music. (*Polly glances at him sharply*) Come on, no-one's going to rape anyone are they?

POLLY Very funny.

MICHAEL takes some beer in a gulp and studies her a moment.

MICHAEL   What's with you tonight? (*Polly shrugs.*
          Michael moves to the table, sits next to her) You
          and Mandy are all matey again, aren't you?
          (*She nods*) So everything's on the up and up,
          right?

POLLY   Wrong.

MICHAEL   Why?

POLLY   Because . . . (*This is hard to get out and she can't*
          quite look at him as she does it) I'm not sure . . .
          there's any point any more. (*Pause*) In us, you
          know.

MICHAEL looks at her a second. There's a genuine hurt, but
fleetingly. He's not going to show it.

MICHAEL   Fair enough.

POLLY   Is that all you can say?

MICHAEL   What do you want me to say? Go all soft all over
          the place? The bended knees routine. No way.

POLLY   I thought you might . . . show you're sorry.
          (*Then*) or something.

MICHAEL   It always comes back to that doesn't it? You
          droning on about what I'm thinking, what I'm
          feeling. (*Then*) Girls!

POLLY   Only because you never want to talk about
          things like that.

MICHAEL   Maybe because I'd feel like a right bloody idiot
          if I did.

POLLY   Why? Because boys aren't supposed to have
          feelings? Aren't allowed to show they might
          care in case people think they're soppy?

MICHAEL'S FACE. If she has a point, he still won't admit it.

MICHAEL   Oh bloody hell . . .

POLLY   You're always laughing at girls, mocking us
because we don't mind showing that we've
got emotions. That makes us pathetic to you,
doesn't it?

MICHAEL   Did I say that? Did I?

POLLY   You didn't have to! Well I'd rather be that way,
any day, than be so . . . worried about my
macho image that I didn't dare feel anything
for anyone!

*It's all come out in a rush, the way these things do, but she's pleased
it's finally out.*

MICHAEL   While we're on about it, it's typical of a girl to
get all bloody pseudo psychological about it!

POLLY'S FACE, angry. She too starts to rise.

MICHAEL   Polly . . . (*She pauses, en route for the door*)
We've had fun haven't we? A laugh. Why can't
it just carry on?

POLLY   (*Simply*) Because it isn't enough.

MICHAEL   What more is there?

POLLY turns to face him.

POLLY   Friendship.

MICHAEL   Come on – we are friends!

POLLY   Friends talk don't they? We're dating. Going
steady, call it what you like. I'm not your friend,
I'm your girlfriend. Never mind I might have
opinions, ideas. So long as I look presentable
and we have a laugh. 'Cos that's what life's
about, after all. One big joke. Or maybe just
I was, for letting you turn me into one.

POLLY goes.

MICHAEL'S FACE. As the front door slams after her, we close in on his expression. Anger there, certainly, but not directed entirely at POLLY. More somehow, at himself, for messing things up.

22   Int. Katherine's Kitchen. Eve.   22

The family, KATHERINE, TERRY and AMANDA and her PARENTS, eating at the table. The BABY, asleep in the carry-cot.

> JUNE   And a christening doesn't have to be anything grand, after all. Just a few relatives, close friends. (*Her voice trails off. Katherine and Terry are exchanging a look*) But of course if you really feel it's something you . . .

KATHERINE   It's alright, Mother. We'll do it.

JUNE'S FACE, at this sudden statement.

FRANK looks at his daughter.

> FRANK   Such enthusiasm. (*As Katherine glances at him*) You make it sound like an act of surrender.

KATHERINE says nothing. Her expression should say it all. Cut to AMANDA, observing.

23   Int. Amanda's Kitchen. Day.   23

A buzz of activity. They are making preparations for food and hospitality to offer guests after the christening.

Everyone is appropriately dressed, and engaged in some chore, from washing up, to setting out sausage rolls on plates.

KATHERINE and TERRY are also present, and the BABY's over KATHERINE's shoulder as she puts out glasses.

JUNE is checking and overseeing the proceedings.

AMANDA What time's the ceremony?

JUNE Three. We should all be back here by four.

FRANK To feed the four thousand by the look of it.

TERRY We're a bit low on the old dry sherry, you want me to nip out to the off-licence?

JUNE Please Terry. (*Then, as Terry leaves, turning to Katherine*) It's time you got changed, Katherine.

KATHERINE Right. (*She bundles the baby into Amanda's arms*) She's all yours. Check her for dampness will you?

AMANDA pulls a face.

We now see that POLLY is also present, and has been roped in, cleaning glasses.

JUNE issues another instruction.

JUNE Amanda, I want you to clean up your bedroom. It looks like a bomb's hit it.

AMANDA (*To her unsuspecting brother who is drinking wine*) Michael? (*As he turns, she shoves the baby into his arms*) You don't mind holding the baby, do you?

Before he can protest, AMANDA and POLLY scuttle out.

MICHAEL Come on – what do I know about babies?

AMANDA (*A parting shot*) Time you learnt, isn't it?

They go, we remain on MICHAEL – ensnared with the infant.

24   Int. Amanda's Hall. Day.   24

POLLY and AMANDA, *en route* up the stairs.

Half-way up they pause, watching MICHAEL through the open doorway, struggling with the BABY.

> POLLY   He's not such a bad bloke.

> AMANDA   She's not such a bad baby. (*Then, with a grin, like an afterthought*) If you like that sort of thing.

POLLY grins back at her, before they move on, up the stairs.

25   Int. Amanda's Bedroom. Day.   25

More activity. There is a black plastic rubbish bag, full to the brim, standing in the middle of the floor. It's chock-a-block with the romantic teenage magazines.

AMANDA and POLLY are stuffing more into it. Charging about the room like mad. Grabbing up the magazines and hurling them into the bag.

> POLLY   And this?

She holds up another magazine.

> AMANDA   All of them. The whole lot.

They continue a moment.

> POLLY   (*In a breathless pause*) You're enjoying this, aren't you?

> AMANDA   And how. (*She stuffs another magazine in*)

And we hold on the crushed and discarded face of PATTI, in the rubbish bag.

26   Int. Kitchen. Day.   26

JUNE, turning as MICHAEL re-enters the kitchen.

MICHAEL is empty handed, except for a glass of wine.

> JUNE   Where's the baby?

> MICHAEL   In her pram. (*Then*) Don't worry. I gave her
> something to look at.

27   Int. Living Room. Day.   27

The BABY is in the pram with a magazine propped up for her
to look at.

28   Int. Living Room. Day.   28

PATTI appears. She begins to talk to the trapped baby.

> PATTI   My, you're a pretty little thing, aren't you? Just
> like a little girl should be. You and I are going
> to see a lot of each other when you grow up.

THE END

A closer look at . . .

Making the future better

Towards the end of *S.W.A.L.K.* Amanda begins to question her future. She realises that having a child and a husband may not be enough – she may feel dissatisfied and unhappy if that were all she had to focus her mind on.

How many people, do you think, feel like June and Frank, Amanda's parents? There seems to be nothing ahead for them. Life has not proved to be as interesting or exciting as they would have wished. In some ways they feel disappointed and let down. Their hopes are now resting on their children, wishing their lives may be more fulfilled.

Life is always going to involve a certain amount of mundane practical reality. There will always be the need to earn a living, and do the routine washing, cooking, and cleaning. We must not expect too much of the people around us. They cannot be interesting, healthy, and entertaining all the time. There will be days when they feel tired, unhappy or ill. So how do we attempt to ensure a satisfying future? How can we all ensure that our lives are as content and full as possible? Is it just a case of having an interesting job and caring, friendly relationships?

There are no definite answers to these questions. We are all individuals in varying circumstances, with different priorities and attitudes. In this last episode of *S.W.A.L.K.* it is suggested that you do not dismiss yourself and you do not allow others to dismiss you. Do not close any doors without thinking about the consequences; leave yourself as many options as possible. This does not just involve ideas about what you can do, but what you think about yourself as well. Do not think that if you are female, all you are capable of is raising children, or that if you are male, this is something you would not be able to do.

Amanda feels that she has begun to sort out what she really wants out of life. She has thrown her piles of 'love' magazines away in an attempt to rid her life of limiting sexist influences. It is a small battle won by Amanda, but has anything changed in the media, advertisements, and people's entrenched attitudes? What influences are there on you? What is causing you to think the way you do?

There is a timely reminder at the end of *S.W.A.L.K.* of the continuous cycle of pressure and influence on people. Patti already has her eye on Katherine's baby. How different is the baby's future going to be? As Patti says, 'You and I are going to see a lot of each other when you grow up'.

TEACHING *S.W.A.L.K.*

Introduction

S.W.A.L.K. could have a useful and entertaining role in many areas of the curriculum. It is a stimulating initiator of both written and discussion work within English. The problems of education, relationships with parents and friends, and dealing with one's own sexuality are common to all young people. It could obviously find a home in Media and Film Studies, especially using both text and video. It could also hold an important place on any Social Studies or Personal and Social Development courses. Teenagers want to talk about growing up, the pressures around them, problems with parents and school, and, of course, sex. It is striking how ill-informed and undeveloped many students' attitudes to sexual relationships can be. *S.W.A.L.K.* is a valuable tool as part of such discussions.

The six episodes are full of material. Much of it your students will find complex and new. The best way to deal with so many issues is to stop after each episode and discuss thoroughly all the ideas involved. I have found that if all six episodes are shown at once the students are often confused about the basic ideas and have forgotten much of what has happened. Treat the episodes in the same way you would a story. Go over interesting or difficult scenes again. *S.W.A.L.K.* easily constitutes half a term's work.

If you are lucky enough to have a video recorder with a good quality still–pause button and slow motion facilities, then make use of them to look at the expressions on characters' faces, discuss how an individual shot was filmed, or to write about the images of youth.

How to use the 'Discussions'

Teenagers often have extremely reactionary and role-bound views of the sexes, and in many cases have never discussed or questioned their own life and future as male or female within society. Research has shown that the most effective way to use material such as *S.W.A.L.K.* is to discuss or outline the issues before watching, and discuss all the issues after watching. (For a good review of the research, see K. Durkin, *Television, Sex Roles and Children*, Open University Press, 1985.)

The discussion pages at the end of each episode are really aimed at the students. They are literally pauses for thought so that the students can talk about and reflect upon some of the ideas in each episode. They can be used in various ways. One of the most successful ways is to break the class up into small groups to discuss the ideas involved, and then bring the groups back together to discuss the main issues. It is not really important to work right through each section of ideas – if a group get caught up talking about the first issue raised, that is fine. I think that emphasis should be placed on issues relating to their own experiences.

S.W.A.L.K. within the curriculum

English/Literature courses

S.W.A.L.K. can be used in the same way as any traditional literature text: watching, reviewing scenes, discussing characters and motivation, and writing about the problems and issues raised by the episodes. It is important here to use the video as the main source of ideas so that students are able to comment on images, tone of voice, and use of music (among other things). The text can be used as a study aid and memory prompt. It is also useful as it enables students to act out for themselves some of the more interesting incidents.

Media courses

S.W.A.L.K. is ideal for use in a Media course because it is about the influence of the media. Fundamental to *S.W.A.L.K.* is the influence the media have in (mis-)representing the two sexes, and the harm this may do to relationships. This is the media concept of representation. Representation is not just a question of presenting stereotypes, but of plot, characters, ideologies, cultural values, and production techniques. This idea can be extended to race and advertising. It is interesting that teenage 'love' magazines make an ideal vehicle for advertisements: they create the market they then sell to the advertiser.

The media are part of what has been termed the 'Consciousness Industry', and in the case of sex roles and teenagers, this is directly related to other industries: make-up, magazines, clothes, music, and so on. The way we look at the world is to a great extent culturally-determined. The culture presented in *S.W.A.L.K.* is geared towards money, even using personal relationships to create 'needs' for products.

Personal/Social Development, Sex Education

S.W.A.L.K. is interesting as it links how things work physically with the emotional, social, and practical sides of relationships. An obvious example of this is the charting of Katherine's pregnancy. We hear about the growing and developing foetus at the same time as seeing Katherine's physical and emotional changes during pregnancy. Amanda plays the role of interested but naive onlooker, constantly having her romantic pre-conceptions dashed by the reality of the situation.

It is a valuable starting point to view experiences of fictional characters such as Amanda and her sister. Most young people will have few qualms commenting upon and discussing such fictional behaviour and problems. It is not a huge step from discussing these problems to relating to them in a more personal way.

Ideas for discussion, written work, and group and individual projects

Episode one: teenage 'love' magazines

1 Research project on 'love' magazines. What type of articles, stories and characters do they contain? Look closely at the images of youth presented and the portrayal of the sexes. What magazines are available? Who owns and publishes them? Who buys them?

2 Advertising within magazines. Ask each member of your group to find an advertisement which they think is either sexist or has in-built values of some kind. Each person could give a short talk about their advert, leading to a general discussion on the nature of advertising – ploys used to sell (playing on people's insecurities, etc). This might, if desired, lead quite naturally to a piece of written work.

3 The value of friendship. What makes a good friend? What causes us to value some people above others? Why so often are our best friends the same sex? Do boys and girls have different interests? If so, what has caused this?

4 Production of a magazine for young people, aiming at both sexes. Problems the group will have to overcome include: what values should it promote? How do you ensure it is popular and interesting without being sexist?

Episode two: the family

1 Research statistics relating to the family. Does the advertiser's dream of Mum, Dad, two children and a dog constitute the majority? Is the number of one-parent families growing? Discuss your findings.

2 Why is society divided up into families? Look at other cultures and social groupings around the world.

3 Who are more important: family or friends?

4 Describe a childhood memory which involves your family and your relationship with them.

5 Write an account of a day in the life of a member of your family in which they describe what it is like to live with you, and what they think and feel about you.

Episode three: education

1 Conduct a class survey on people's favourite subjects and the ones they feel they perform best in. Analyse the results. Can your findings be divided into different results for different sexes? Are there any subjects which do not appear for girls? Boys?

2 Compare your parents' education with your own. What has changed, and what has not?

3 Is school sexist? Do teachers treat boys and girls differently or have different expectations of them? Do boys get told off more often, or in a different way? Are girls expected to be quieter and better-mannered?

4 Look through your school books: what image of women and men do they present? Are females less often shown in books, more likely to be passive, and less likely to have an important role?

Episode four: sexual relationships

1 Project on methods of birth control. Discuss the values and problems with each form of birth control, including the medical effects and the issue of which partner assumes responsibility for precautions.

2 Linking birth control to a concept of personal morality: this is often difficult as a group of teenagers will usually encompass such a range of experience and maturity, but it is well worth discussing. An interesting starting point is to look at the age of consent and discuss its nature, the reasoning behind it, and its relevance.

3 Discuss the nature of attraction between people. Write a list of aspects of another person which cause us to find them attractive. Put this list of qualities in order of importance. Then debate priorities: how important should appearance be, and so on.

4 A close look at sex education. Who should teach young people about sex? How? What exactly should sex education include? What is the best age for sex education? The group (or volunteers) could be asked to describe how they have learned or are learning about sex.

Episode five: marriage

1 Research project into marriage and divorce. For example: how old are people who get married? Are people who marry younger more likely to get divorced? How many divorces are there each year? You might compare modern day trends with statistics from the past. (Your local reference library may be able to supply useful statistics . . .) Discuss the implications of your research.

2 Personal interviews with an elderly couple (parents, grandparents, neighbours) who have been married for a long time. Take time preparing questions and then analysing responses.

3 A close analysis of Frank and June's relationship. How good/bad is it? What are the problems and why?

4 Look at marriage in other cultures. Other societies don't always expect people to choose their partners on the grounds of love. What criteria do they have for choosing partners? Alternatively, explore marriages in the past. An interesting but fairly advanced book on the subject is Lawrence Stone, *Family, Sex and Marriage in England, 1500–1800*, which looks at changing attitudes.

Episode six: making the future better

1 Ask the class to make individual projections into their own future. What would they like to happen to them in the next ten years? These ideas can then be discussed in small groups or a full class as a debate. Ask them to examine any differences in the ideas of girls and boys. If there are any differences (eg. more girls seeing having children as an ambition), they could explore why this might be so.

2 Look closely at Amanda. What has changed about her by the end of *S.W.A.L.K.* and why? Can you relate any of her problems to your life?

3 Thinking ahead to being a parent. How will you bring up your children? What sort of world do you want them to grow up in?

Useful addresses

Advisory Centre for Education 18 Victoria Park, London.
Tel (01) 980 4596
Free advice on questions of law in education, discrimination in education, sex education etc. Leaflets available.

British Pregnancy Advisory Service Austy Manor, Woolton Warren, Solihull, West Midlands. Tel (05642) 3225
Advice and help on pregnancy, contraceptives and abortion. Pregnancy testing. Contact the above address for your nearest branch.

Citizens Advice Bureau Address of local branch in telephone directory. Free advice on a wide range of issues – employment, welfare, benefits and family matters.

Careers Research and Advisory Centre (CRAC) Sheraton House, Castle Park, Cambridge CB3 0AX. Tel (0223) 460277
Organises courses and conferences on careers for careers teachers and Sixth Formers.
For individual careers advice, see *Education Authority*.

Education Authority Look in the telephone directory for your local education authority to arrange an appointment for free and independent careers' advice.

Equal Opportunities Commission Overseas House, Quay Street, Manchester. Tel (061) 833 9244
Useful leaflets, and information on how to obtain videos on choosing a career, leaving school, training schemes, equality at school and work, etc.

Family Planning Association (Head Office) 27–35 Mortimer Street, London W1N 7RJ. Tel (01) 636 7866
Free leaflets and advice. Look in the telephone directory for your *local clinic*. Confidential advice, help and treatment on contraception and pregnancy available.

Sexually Transmitted Disease (STD) Clinics
Look in the telephone directory under *Sexually Transmitted Disease* or *Venereal Disease* or your local hospital.
Free and confidential advice, help and treatment for AIDS and sexually-transmitted diseases.

Society for Education in Film and Television (SEFT)
29 Old Compton Street, London W1V 5PL. Tel (01) 734 5455
Advice, information and seminars on media education.

Terrence Higgins Trust BM/AIDS, London WC1N 3XX.
Tel (01) 833 2971
Advice and help to people with AIDS, and to their friends and relatives. Gives detailed information and leaflets.

Further reading

Jane Cousins, *Make it Happy*, Penguin, 1986

Angela McRobie and Trish McCabe, *Feminism for Girls: An Adventure Story*, Routledge and Kegan Paul, 1981

Angela Phillips and Jill Rakusen, *Our Bodies, Ourselves*, Penguin 1978